INDIA

AS

KNOWLEDGE

SOCIETY

Institution – Enterprise Perspectives

C BHAKTAVATSALA RAO

LEADERCREST ACADEMY

notionpress.com

INDIA · SINGAPORE · MALAYSIA

ISBN 979-8-89277-978-4

Contents

Section 1
Institutional Perspectives

Section 2
Enterprise Perspectives

Foreword

Although the phrase "Incredible India" has been coined only a few years ago, India had always been incredible. The scientific and technical thought that went into the centuries' old Indian heritage of Ayurveda, Yoga, Astronomy, and Architecture (especially temple and palace architecture) was indeed phenomenal.

India may not have been able to participate in the first three industrial revolutions having been under successive foreign occupations. Post-independence in 1947, however, India has been catching up progressively on the knowledge canvas. From the 1950s, India demonstrated rare pluck to construct its own massive dams, build its own heavy industry, establish its own banks and financial institutions, develop its own educational infrastructure, and create its own aerospace infrastructure.

India may not have gained immediate global competitiveness, but the country certainly and quickly acquired the capability for self-reliance and self-sufficiency across a range of basic and heavy industries that is rare amongst the emerging markets. This was followed up with global leadership in software and information technology services.

Simultaneously, India also expanded and reinforced its higher academic and research strengths with Indian Institutes of Technology, National Institutes of Technology, Indian Institutes of Information Technology, Indian Institutes of Management, and scores of universities, colleges, and educational institutions. India also established several scientific research institutions. Governmental investments played a major role in the academic renaissance.

India is today poised to be third largest economy globally by 2028. India is also now passionate about building new industrial sinews in sunrise sectors such as renewables, semiconductors, sensors, electric batteries, electronics and several other such domains.

This book presents important perspectives covering the broad topic of India as Knowledge Society. The book has 22 chapters which are divided into two sections – Institutional Perspectives and Enterprise Perspectives. Some of the chapters are based on my thoughts of mid-2000s. These are included in the book, with minor updates, to demonstrate the importance of futurism.

The book will be of interest to academicians, students, administrators, policy makers and professionals. As India becomes a knowledge society with multiple initiatives as discussed in this book, India would further reinforce its global economic standing.

The views expressed in this book, including those related to educational institutions or enterprises, are my personal views and do not necessarily represent the views of any institution or enterprise with which I was or am associated.

As always, I will be happy to receive feedback from the readers on cbrao2005@gmail.com.

C Bhaktavatsala Rao

April 01, 2024

List of Figures

Other Books by the Author

As C B Rao

From Start-up to Ramp up: Indian Context and Global Insights

Technology and Competitive Strategy: Strategies for Innovators, Differentiators and Followers

Competitive Strategy: A Contemporary Retake

Leadership for India Inc.: An Experiential Treatise

India as Global Start-up Hub: Mission with Passion

India's Economic Resurgence: A Modified Paradigm for a Welfare State

Work-Life Balance: Essays in Individual and Organizational Behaviour

Product Strategy and Corporate Success: Concepts and Cases from the Indian Automobile Industry

Strategic Management: Practice and Philosophy for India Inc.

STEM: Strategy. Technology. Entrepreneurship. Management

As C Bhaktavatsala Rao

Legendary Leaders: Insights and Lessons

Dharmic Management: Lessons from the Indian Social Ecosystem

Strategic Marketing: Cases and Concepts from the Indian Business

Personal Mastery: Competence-Behaviour Frameworks

Organizational Mastery: Competence-Behaviour Frameworks

Institutional Perspectives

Chapter 1

Globalization of the IITs

A Pan-IIT 2008 Thought Stream

The Indian Institutes of Technology (IITs) are the most visible symbols of India's prowess in scientific and technical education. Alumni of the IITs have distinguished themselves in academic and industrial settings in India and in all the advanced countries of the world. IITs have also joined global rankings, apart from emerging at the top in the Indian national rankings (National Institute of Ranking Framework of the Ministry of Education, Government of India). No wonder then that there is a discussion, time to time, on what else the IITs could or should do on a global canvas. Here are a few thoughts.

Commercializing cutting-edge research

As of 2023, the IIT system has completed 73 years of high technology educational saga in India. What started as an undergraduate program soon became a beacon for higher order postgraduate and research education. It is a matter of no mean significance that Ph.D. students constitute about 20-25 percent of the total student population in the IITs. Postgraduate and research education has been an engine of growth in the IITs. Centres in areas of cutting-edge science and technology such as biotechnology, nanotechnology, robotics, brain research, and artificial intelligence have been established.

Innovative ideas and inventions began to be generated and incubated as entrepreneurial start-ups, primarily through adjunct research parks (IIT Madras Research Park being the leader). This model has been perfected in the United States by several universities and is also pioneered in Europe by institutes such as Karolinska Institute. This model can be easily executed by the IITs in India. Following the example set by IIT Madras, Research Parks were set up by various IITs. These ventures were appropriately supported by government grants, alumni contributions, and industrial donations so that faculty and inventive students are enabled in their entrepreneurial journeys.

Converging engineering and medicine

For far too long a period, India has treated Engineering and Medicine as two physically and intellectually distinct streams of education and research. This contrasts sharply with the US scenario where the best engineering and medical institutions function within common campuses, and under shared umbrellas. With advances in genetic engineering, medical engineering, physical, chemical, and material sciences, and several hybrid domains, it has become possible to study the human body (or objects of life) as much as engineering traditionally studied inanimate objects (such as buildings or machinery). The goal of science and engineering will be to understand life in its entirety to be able to arrive at cost-effective diagnostic and therapeutic solutions.

To promote such convergence, IITs need to expand curriculum to include biological sciences as well as hybrid biology-engineering domains to create requisite academic and research platforms. Indian Institute of Science and IIT Madras have taken the lead in this regard. This initiative needs to be broadened. Just as management schools have become integral parts of the IITs, medical schools would also need to be parts of IITs. Medical undergraduates need to be facilitated to acquire postgraduate engineering degrees in fields such as robotic surgery, tele-medicine, bio-medical engineering, artificial intelligence, and so on. Similarly, engineering undergraduates should be facilitated to acquire postgraduate medical degrees in fields such as genetic engineering, artificial organ engineering, pharmaceutical drug delivery, human biotechnology, and medical nanotechnology, and so on. Figure 1.1 summarises initiatives for promoting convergence of sciences and engineering at IITs.

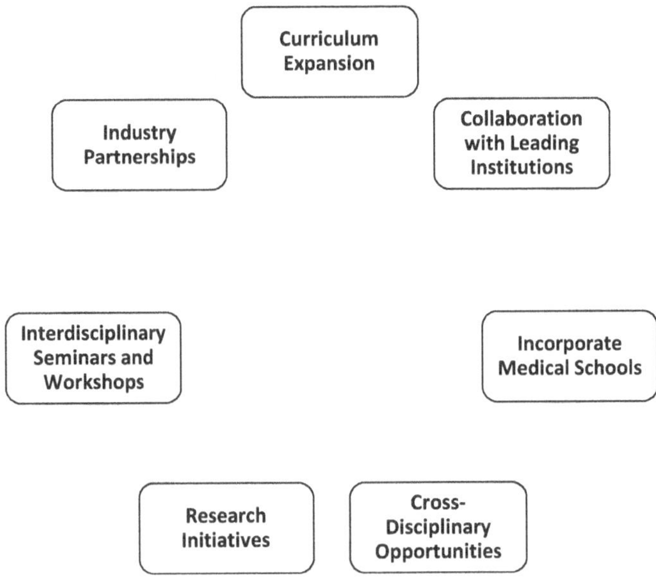

Figure 1.1: Initiatives for Promoting Convergence of Sciences and Engineering at IITs

Globalization of IITs

IIT alumni have been the most powerful and iconic representatives of India's highly successful IIT system abroad. Despite the clear knowledge and competence edge, IITs have not been overtly successful in drawing students from advanced countries. Even students from emerging economies and contiguous nations are not many at the IITs. Lack of awareness, geopolitical vagaries, family and cultural issues, logistics, higher costs of overseas education and loss of linkages with employment sources could be the causes that limit the number of students accessing IITs in India. The only way to irrefutably strengthen IITs' global blueprint is only through physical presence in advanced countries.

This could, at the minimum level, take the shape of faculty collaboration cum student exchange programs with reputed overseas institutions and, at the aspirational level, could involve setting up of overseas campuses. Here again, IIT Madras has taken the lead with its first international campus in Tanzania. The latter strategy, of course, requires deep financial resources and support of non-resident Indians in a big way. Another start could be made with the setting up of mini campuses within major universities such as Harvard, Stanford, MIT, Oxford, Cambridge and Karolinska. The value proposition for those universities would be in terms of an intense exposure to Indian economic, scientific, technical, and business perspectives and preparation of their students for cross-cultural professional employment.

Strengthening the faculty

Even as the intake of IITs has been expanding, the share of research by the IITs growing and the number of IITs itself increasing, the availability of requisite faculty has become a major issue. There is a need to create new tiers of post-doctoral programs to generate and retain new pools of academically oriented researchers who could undertake a variety of educational and research activities in the IITs. At another level, apart from enhancing the compensation levels for the faculty members, and increasing their share of consultancy income, out-of-box measures such as participation in research driven start-ups could attract greater number of bright doctoral and post-doctoral professionals to the IITs.

The Government of India and University Grants Commission have announced multiple initiatives to create the positions of chair professors, adjunct faculty, and professors of practice to attract and create pools of superannuated faculty as well as industry professionals for teaching application-oriented courses. Such professors would be well-suited to conceptualise and run executive development programmes. However, enough care must be taken to ensure that high standards of industrial and business practices are brought into the institutions as part of these initiatives. Passion for knowledge sharing on the part of the aspirants to the professorial positions would be essential.

Transactional efficiency in consulting

IITs can help industries and businesses, big and small, in problem-solving and growth-planning through science and technology. This is because of the superior laboratory resources, computer facilities and knowledge systems that reside in the IITs. The vast pool of students and researchers can, of course, undertake project works of short duration. However, the IITs have not been able to leverage these intellectual assets due to slow pace of consulting transactions. With additional focus on business development and project management, the IITs can achieve expanded scope and transactional efficiency. Consulting at the IITs should, however, be truly in knowledge-intensive sectors befitting the scientific pedigree.

Deployment of modern electronic and telecommunication technologies in logistics and transportation projects could, for example, be a challenging area of consultancy. Design of flexible manufacturing systems for small and medium enterprises could be another. Democratisation of artificial intelligence would be an important futuristic area. There would be many potential areas in each of industrial, business, and administrative sectors that demand the skillsets of the IITs. By focusing on and commercializing cutting-edge research, integrating engineering and medicine, globalizing the campus presence and faculty-student intake, reinforcing the faculty, and enhancing transactional efficiency in consulting, the IITs would become the top-tier educational system on a global basis over the next two decades. Figure 1.2 summarises the strategies to achieve transactional efficiency.

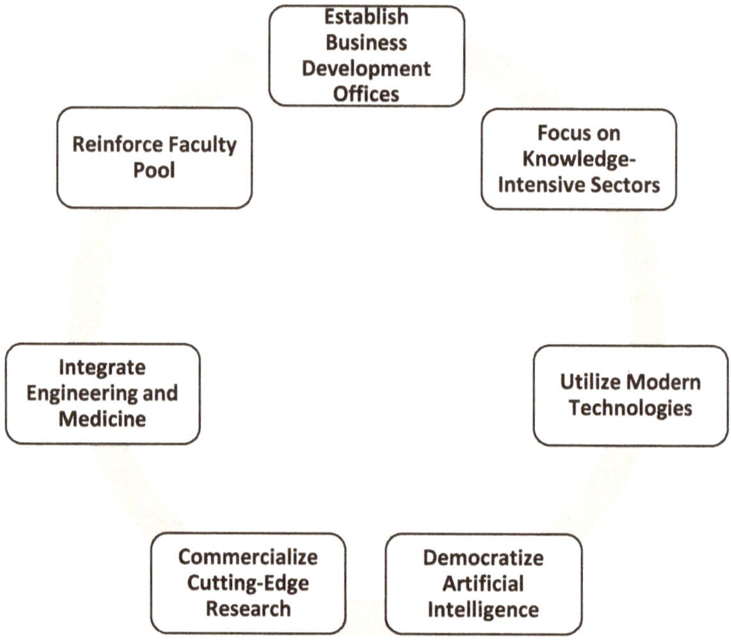

Figure 1.2: Strategies to Achieve Transactional Efficiency

Chapter 2

Like IAS, IES, IFS etc.

Needed: Indian Directorial Service (IDS)

Corporate frauds wherever and whenever they occur, from Enron in US to Satyam in India, bring focus, multiple times, on the role of independent directors on the boards of companies. Several white papers on the collapse of Enron pointed out that lax regulatory environment and poor oversight by the Enron board contributed to the fraud in and collapse of the company. Regulations have since been tightened up significantly, reporting requirements enhanced substantially and oversight expectations on boards escalated notably in the major economies of the world. In all this effort, major emphasis has been placed on having a higher proportion of independent directors in the boards. This focus on independent directors has not helped matters as evidenced by the successive corporate failures in various jurisdictions.

Directors' independence: real or apparent?

In India, Clause 49 of the Listing Agreement with the Stock Exchanges specifies the role and requirements of independent directors on the boards of listed companies. SEBI has recently introduced Business Responsibility and Social Responsibility (BRSR) reporting, incorporating strong elements of Environmental, Social and Governance (ESG) reporting. These are positive and comprehensive initiatives. From time to time, however, despite the well-meaning regulations and the institution of independent directors, deliberate frauds and systemic deficiencies continue to exist in some wayward companies. This is exemplified by not only the corporate frauds of the past but also some of the more recent cases of corporate insolvency.

Satyam, for example, had some of the most talented and respected names as the independent directors on its board, prior to the blowout of the misgovernance episodes. The list included Mr V P Rama Rao, former Chief Secretary to the Government of Andhra Pradesh, Dr (Mrs) Mangalam Srinivasan, Adviser to Kennedy School of Government, Harvard, Professor Krishna Palepu of Harvard Business School, Mr Vinod Dham, the famous Intel chip discoverer, Professor M Rammohan Rao of Indian School of Business, Mr T R Prasad, a former cabinet secretary, Government of India and Professor V S Raju of Indian Institute of Technology Madras/ Delhi. The number of independent directors at 7 was larger than the number of whole-time directors at 3. The company was listed on NYSE and therefore was subject to the most rigorous reporting requirements of Sarbanes-Oxley Act of the USA.

Tracing the faults

From an analysis of Satyam's corporate governance report, the independent directors participated in the board meetings as well as in the governance committees such as audit committee in full compliance of the then existing corporate governance norms. The directors represented proven, distilled administrative, technological, management, governance, and academic experience. The company had a full-fledged Code of Conduct and Ethics for Directors. None of the above has, however, helped the board or the independent directors of Satyam, individually or as a group, to detect the corporate fraud that happened under the board's very nose. It is indeed ironic that one of the independent directors of Satyam, Professor Krishna Palepu had the distinction of co-authoring with Professor Paul Healy of Harvard Business School a landmark book titled "The Fall of Enron" in 2003!

Obviously, there is more than individual expertise and integrity that is on test under the independent director system.

The fault does not lie in the independent directors, per se. The very act of having professionals at the peak of their respective careers or at the launch of new careers post-retirement as independent directors brings with it the issue of time constraint. In the few hours they have at their disposal for each board meeting, such directors can bring no more than a whiff of world's best practices or a gentle advice of caution to the deliberations of the boards. They would have neither the time nor the capability to analyse projects, operations, plans and finances to detect systematic fraudulent activities. The problem of inadequate attention gets compounded as such reputed professionals are much sought after as outside directors in several companies. In addition, there could be dependence on promoters for continued board tenure, which may influence independence.

Talent pool for directors

India has several thousand joint stock companies out of which nearly 6,000 are listed on India's oldest stock exchange, Bombay Stock Exchange. If these board managed companies require 5 to 7 independent directors each (based on an average board size of 10, with 2 to 3 members being whole-time directors and 2 members representing investors) there is a gigantic requirement for 30,000 to 35,000 independent directors to guide and manage these listed companies. It would be self-defeating to try to source them from a professional pool which is otherwise engaged in fulltime work of its own. If one superimposes the need for such independent directors to contribute effectively to the affairs of the company through industry knowledge, strategic guidance, operational oversight, and risk management as well as in regulatory compliance, internal audit and management audit, the job of independent directors becomes a fulltime job with specific skill sets. The problem is not confined to private sector alone; several public sector companies also face the problem.

To make the boards truly perceptive and powerful bodies, with independent directors making a distinctive knowledge cum practice-based contribution to the functioning of the boards, major structural and systemic changes in the institution of independent directors are called for. As illustrated in Figure 2.1, there are four aspects to this: (a) creation of a dedicated all-India talent pool for independent directors, (b) making the independent directors truly independent and empowered, (c) integrating the independent directors in the strategic functioning of the company, and (d) making the remuneration of independent directors non-discretionary. These objectives can be fulfilled by the creation of an Indian Directorial Service (IDS) on the lines of the famed Indian Administrative Service (IAS) which creditably runs the Indian government.

Figure 2.1: Reforming Independent Director Roles: Four Key Aspects

Indian Directorial Service

IDS will be a special, high profile corporate cadre selected, trained, placed, and compensated by the Government of

India through its entities. The selection to IDS will be made through an all-India selection process by a newly created Union Corporate Directors Commission (UCDC) akin to the Union Public Services Commission (UPSC). The training for the directors selected for IDS will be carried out by a newly created National Corporate Directors Academy (NCDA) akin to the National Defence Academy (NDA) in collaboration with the various Indian Institutes of Management and Management departments of the Indian Institutes of Technology as well as other reputed management institutions. All these institutions will be encouraged to set up academic verticals for corporate directors. The placement of independent directors from the IDS in various companies will be made by a Standing Committee for Independent Directors (SCID) under the governance of SEBI. The compensation for the independent directors will be carved out of a share of post-tax (pre-dividend distribution) earnings reported by the corporate entities and administered by the Ministry of Corporate Affairs (MCA), if necessary, through the National Company Law Tribunal (NCLT).

Requirements and expectations

Unlike the IAS and other public services, the minimum entry age for IDS will be 40 years of age with a minimum of post-graduate qualification and 15 years of senior level industrial, business, academic, administrative or armed forces experience. Maximum age of entry will be 60 years. Superannuation age will be 80 years, extendable on special considerations for persons of eminence and in good health. Senior executives from private and public sector companies as well as universities will be encouraged to apply. Aptitude, attitude, and knowledge tests appropriate to directorial responsibilities will be administered as part of the selection process. The selection will be national and conducted annually. The tenure will typically be for renewable terms of 5 years and subject to the usual shareholder approvals. The IDS pool will be typically rotated across companies and industries to promote cross-fertilization of ideas and avoid the development of vested interests.

The independent directors are expected to guide and influence the boards to make objective and ethical quarterly and annual reports to the shareholders, stock exchanges, SEBI, SCID, and MCA about the companies they manage. The reports will be strategic in nature and cover critical aspects such as business environment facing the company, competitiveness of the company, performance parameters and ratio analysis, regulatory compliance, SHE (safety, health and environmental), ESG and BRSR profiles, risk and prudential management and human resource accounting. Each of the independent directors on the board is expected to take a lead role in each of the 7 areas. One of the independent directors shall be appointed as the Chairperson or Vice-Chairperson of the company.

It is expected that each independent director from IDS will not be on the boards of more than two companies and not be on the board of more than one company from the same industry. Each independent director will have a working office as well as a basic secretariat in the company and possess the freedom to operate fulltime or halftime in the company, depending on whether the person has one or two board memberships. The independent directors will be provided access to the management information system (MIS) of the company and will be afforded the freedom to interact with the senior tier of executives directly reporting to the CEO. The independent directors will be bound by standard confidentiality and non-compete covenants.

A total talent source

When IDS takes off on the lines suggested above, it may evolve from being a governance cadre to a becoming a total talent source for directorships in the companies. It may lead to a healthy competition between the home-grown whole-time directors and the externally inducted independent directors. Companies would have the benefit of a knowledge-driven, fully functional board contributing to all aspects of corporate management.

Obviously, for a major structural initiative such as IDS to succeed, this new public service must be provided with the necessary legal enablement. Necessary supportive institutions such as UCDC, NCDA, SCID discussed here should be established. MCA and NCLT as well as SEBI should be expanded to be able to handle additional administrative responsibilities efficiently. Apex industry associations such as Confederation of Indian Industry (CII) and management institutions should lend their full support to the concept. Indian Directorial Service could be a major structural and systemic reform that could be a pioneering one even globally. Figure 2.2 summarises the key success factors for IDS.

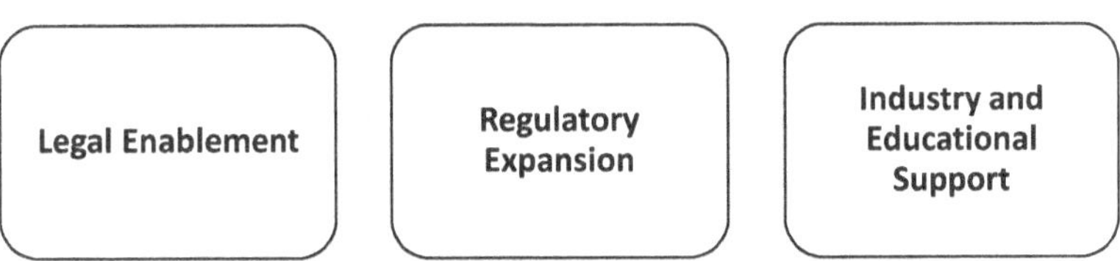

Figure 2.2: Key Success Factors for the Indian Directorial Service (IDS)

Chapter 3

Life Science Technologies

The Next Frontier for the IITs

The Indian Institute of Technology Madras (IITM) organized on August 14, 2010, a symposium titled "Medical Education and Research in Independent India: A Critical Review and Projected Role of IITs in Post-graduate Medical Education and Research" at its campus. Apart from the Director of IITM, Professor M S Ananth, two eminent medical professionals, Professor B M Hegde (a noted cardiologist, former vice-chancellor of Manipal University and a recipient of the Padma Bhushan award) and Dr C V Krishnaswamy (a renowned diabetologist and a pioneer in affordable diabetes treatment for the needy through the Voluntary Health Services, Chennai) delivered critical review lectures. An eminent chemist, Dr Lalitha and a reputed physicist Dr Srinivasan provided additional perspectives as panellists.

Open issues

The symposium raised several open issues with the very relevance and appropriateness of modern medicine as taught and practised coming under serious critique by the two distinguished invitees. Both the speakers are well-known for their erudition as well as campaign against certain practices of exploitative medicine. Both the speakers consider the human body as a technological energy-house, capable of rewiring itself and requiring only a minimalist medical or surgical intervention. Not surprisingly Professor Ananth remarked that he stood confused after listening to their lectures. If the symposium was intended to lay a charter for the

IITs in medical education, the purpose was far from accomplished. Yet, the very act of focusing on the potential role of the IITs in medical education was a ground-breaking thought. Dr Ananth deserves kudos for germinating and pursuing this thought, which has since been realized in 2022-23 with medical schools being established in the Indian Institute of Science, Bengaluru and Indian Institute of Technology Madras, Chennai.

The proposition of medical education in the IITs appeared counter-intuitive in 2010 given that the IITs had been established solely for excellence in higher technological education and research. The proposition appeared to go against the Indian educational eco-system which, for decades, saw engineering and medicine as two distinct (and almost non-complementary) streams of education. So much so, at school finishing level itself the students were being required to choose between a mathematics-physics-chemistry stream, which was a prerequisite for engineering education, and a biology-physics-chemistry stream, which was a pre-requisite for medical education. Given the resource scarcity in higher education in India it was also debatable then if additional resources of the IITs should be spent on diversifying into medical education and research or on deepening the core competencies in scientific and technological education and research. At that time, I posted a blog making a strong case for analysing the proposal with due objectivity and going forward on the path of harnessing the synergy between engineering and medicine, in a futuristic way. I am delighted that the confluence of medical science and technology has now become a reality. I wish to recall through this chapter the salient points that I raised in 2010 on this matter, with some contemporary updates.

The macro-case for the IITs

The Indian Institutes of Technology (IITs) are a group of 23 autonomous engineering and technology-oriented institutes of higher education, established and declared as Institutes of National Importance by the Parliament of India, and hence established directly by the Central government. The IITs were created to train scientists and engineers, with the aim of developing a skilled workforce to support the economic and social development of India after independence in 1947. In the order of establishment, they are located in Kharagpur (1950; as IIT 1951), Mumbai (1958), Chennai, formerly Madras (1959), Kanpur (1959), Delhi (1961; as IIT 1963), Guwahati (1994), Roorkee (1847; as IIT 2001), Ropar (2008), Bhubaneswar (2008), Gandhinagar (2008), Hyderabad (2008), Patna (2008), Jodhpur (2008), Indore (2009), Mandi (2009), Varanasi (1919; as IIT 2012), Dhanbad (1926; as IIT 2016), Palakkad (2015), Tirupati (2015), Bhilai (2016), Dharwad (2016), Jammu (2016), and Goa (2016). Some of the earlier IITs were established with financial assistance and technical expertise from UNESCO, Germany, the United States, Japan, and the Soviet Union.

Each IIT is an autonomous university, linked to the others through a common IIT Council, which oversees their administration. They have a common admission process for undergraduate admissions, using the Joint Entrance Examination (popularly known as IIT-JEE) to select around 10,000 undergraduate candidates a year. Postgraduate admissions are done based on the national competitive examinations called GATE, JMET, JAM and CEED. According to data provided by the Education Ministry in Parliament, more than 25,000 students from IITs were set to graduate in the 2022-23 academic year. The alumni of the IITs have become top-ranking scientists, technologists, managers, and entrepreneurs globally. The IITs, especially the ones with long history, have won consistent ratings among the top technological institutions of the world. In more ways than one, the IITs have become global institutions and brands of India, attracting the best students and teachers in India.

Higher medical education

In contrast, higher medical education in India has largely been introverted, partly due to the institutional constraints and partly due to the reluctance of advanced economies to open to foreign doctors. Neither has it been promoted as an educational mission of national importance by the Central government as it did in the case of IITs. There are only a few national medical institutions such as AIIMS and JIPMER in a few locations, which are centrally sponsored. Most other medical institutions are State sponsored or private sponsored and have won reputation as teaching hospitals. New AIIMS and other apex medical institutions that are coming up follow the established template. If the concept of IITs as institutes of national importance has paid off, an analogous concept in medical education as a mission of national importance should be equally relevant and feasible. By extending the scope of IITs to include medical education, potentially the seven-decade plus experience and institutional structure of the IITs can be effectively leveraged for medical education.

Science, technology, and medicine

The other logical premise relates to the role of science and engineering in the field of medicine. From diagnostics to surgery, and from pharmaceuticals to human organs, technology plays a major role as never before. The body scanning and blood analysis equipment and processes are getting advanced each year with more sophisticated imaging systems, informatics, and predictive capability. As the sciences of human genetics and genetic engineering become more advanced the ability to predict likely disease incidence and therapeutic efficacy would only increase in future. At the other end of the spectrum, minimally invasive surgical methods, utilizing robotics and laser surgery on one hand and regenerative medicine including transfused and auto stem cell therapies would substitute the classic surgical scalpel. Artificial Intelligence is another, all-encompassing, futuristic force. In more senses than one, future physicians and surgeons need to be expert biologists, physicists, chemists, engineers, and technologists, all rolled into one. This indeed is a tough call and requires a highly communicative, collaborative, and networked community of scientists and technologists.

By letting the current graduate studies in sciences, engineering and medicine consolidate as at present but establishing a new paradigm of postgraduate and research studies in life science technologies, the IITs can certainly make biology and technology work for medicine. The challenge is, therefore, not merely one of teaching medicine in the IITs; it is one of defining a whole new stream of life sciences technology. This would involve understanding the human body better through deployment of engineering tools, individualizing diagnosis and therapeutics through deployment of genetics, real-time imaging of all the body organs with near-zero radioactive load, potentiating pharmaceuticals through newer molecular moieties, more patient-friendly and more efficacious delivery systems, moving surgery into an almost non-invasive technological tool, regenerating the human body through its own immune and cellular therapeutics, and making artificial intelligence near-natural intelligence. IITs can certainly create these new life science technological substrates through higher education and research. Respecting that human beings can never arrogate themselves to create or modify life, which is God's great creation, some of the potential lifecycle technological theorems are hypothesized below in Figure 3.1.

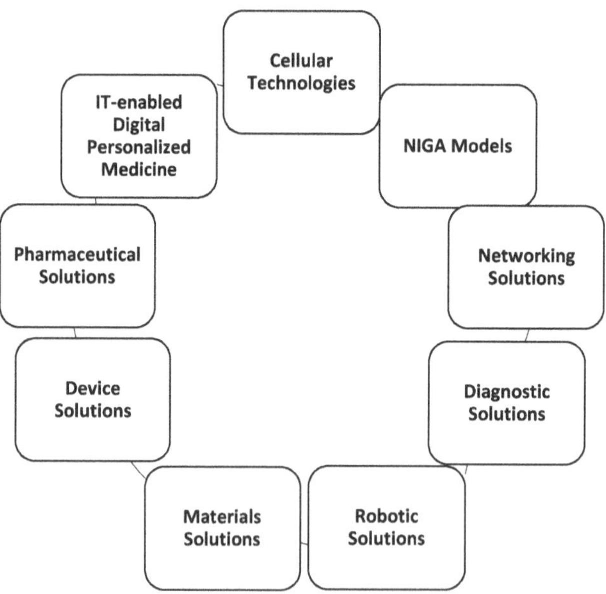

Figure 3.1: Potential Lifecycle Technological Theorems

Modelling the human body and mind

Cellular technologies. Engineering aims to reduce the abstract to precise, visualize the hidden and optimize performance. From mathematical equations to heuristic algorithms, and from simulation to fuzzy logic, multiple engineering approaches are available to model systems. Biological and medical sciences have so far used in vitro and in vivo animal models to understand how human body gets affected by disease and how it is cured by medicines. This modelling continues to be the principal theme of medical development despite the knowledge that exists that animal modelling does not simulate, replicate, or predict human modelling. If the fundamental building block of human body, or for that matter any living organism, the "cell" is understood better the science of life and living becomes stronger. Considering that the human body is made of trillions of cells as building blocks, with different types of cells conducting different tasks, modelling, engineering, and optimizing cellular behaviour is the fundamental challenge as well as opportunity for newer life science technologies.

NIGA models. Engineering has moved from designing and manufacturing machines operated by human beings to designing, manufacturing and operating human-like machines, the humanoids. Science has moved from explaining the laws of physics, chemistry, and biology to cloning and creating biological organisms leveraging the laws that have been discovered and defined. Yet, what propels cells to do what they do has not been understood yet. The nutrition-immunity-growth-aging (NIGA) model (an acronym coined by me) has not been understood either as an individual model or collective system. Energy is essential for growth; yet it is not understood at what points of time, and in which manners, energy supply to, and consumption by, the human body become optimal or sub-optimal. Relating cell growth and death to alternative models of nutrition and energy would be an essential component of life science technologies. IITs, having mastered mechanical, electrical, electronics and computer engineering domains can apply these principles to establish and validate customized NIGA models at cellular levels.

Networking solutions. The human body is an impossibly complex electro-mechanical, neuron-capillary network with multiple biological sensors, pumps and filters that maintain the body and mind in harmony with themselves and in dynamic equilibrium with an often-hostile environment. Principles of engineering can be utilized to model these interactions. For example, failure of venous pumps in legs causes accumulation of blood in capillaries and swelling of either peripheral or deep veins. Engineering rather than medical solutions to correct the pumping abnormalities are perhaps called for. Mapping of brain exteriors as well as interiors in neurologically challenged persons, and reviving of neural networks in brains of stroke-incapacitated patients is yet another area where electrical engineering could offer relevant solutions.

Diagnostic solutions. Clearly, major strides have been taken in developing diagnostic equipment which produce highly granulated images of the human body based on computer, magnetic resonance, and positive emission aided scanning devices. While the typical current equipment is minimally invasive and much faster compared to the earlier generation equipment, the continued use of radiation and radiological contrasting agents bring in risks of invasive analysis and discomfort. It is necessary to work on continued engineering solutions which not only sharpen the imaging capabilities but also correlate with clinical outcomes in auto diagnosis as well as in feedback correction model.

Robotic solutions. The use of robots for surgery has indeed been a game changer. Large incisions have now given way to keyhole surgeries. Use of robots in surgery go a step further as new technologies enable slender, flexible arms to navigate through the contoured internals of the human body. While so far robots have provided better magnification, precision, and manipulative skills in one-to-one relationship with surgeons, it is possible to envisage a future whereby more than one robot could be pressed into service to perform multiple tasks simultaneously. It is also possible to envisage miniaturized robots and nano robots which can be placed in the internal body systems for tracking and catering to more precise nature of body responses during the surgical processes.

Materials solutions. From creation of synthetic organs to development of artificial blood, engineering can play a major role. Discovery and development of more bio-compatible materials together with in situ design and manufacture of required human parts could lead to better outcomes, especially in orthopaedic, cardiac, and cosmetic surgeries. Materials which minimize blood loss, suturing systems which promote rapid self-healing, carriers and excipients that enable better bioavailability for pharmaceuticals are all within the realms of engineering possibility.

Pharmaceutical solutions. IITs have a great track record in the sciences of chemistry and physics. Chemistry is traditionally focused on engineering kinetics and dynamics in a machine system rather than on kinetics and dynamics of molecules in a human system. Yet, these two key disciplines, can be supplemented to develop powerhouses of new chemical entities and new drug delivery systems. With the addition of newer disciplines of biotechnology and nanotechnology, the IITs are well positioned to conduct drug discovery and drug development activities in both small molecule and large molecules spaces.

Device solutions. Medical devices are increasingly playing a major role in administering multiple injectable medicines simultaneously and monitoring patient condition, bedside. The ultimate destination of this quest should be to have a patch which when worn on the patient's skin can provide a complete readout of all the body parameters. New biochemistry and bio-enzyme technologies would be required which could apply principles of microporosis and generate inputs to a wide range of conditions like salt and electrolyte balances in the body. This coupled with devices which are capable of programming, feedback and self-regulation could take medicine to an auto-management mode.

IT-enabled digital personalized medicine. The IITs, decades ago, pioneered computer education. They also have been the pioneers in mathematical and stochastic modelling as well as application of statistics and economics. All these capabilities can be applied for developing new frontiers of personalized digital medicine to eliminate variability in person-to-person therapeutic efficacy. A host of clinical and medical sciences such as pharmaco-genomics, pharmaco-economics, genetic prescription, and personalized medicine can be expanded based on application of computer sciences. From simple archiving and analysis of clinical data to complex predictive modelling, IITs can harness their digital hardware and software skills to enable personalized medicine.

The above are only a few illustrative areas indicative of the capability of engineering to redefine higher medical education and research.

Life science technologies – actions for the IITs

Clearly, there are a number of domains and applications where the principles of engineering and physical sciences, including mathematics, when combined with the principles of biological sciences can provide breakthrough solutions for medical needs that are unmet or can be met in a better manner. Clearly the current medical schools which have no engineering background are not the campuses to aim for such new developments. On the other hand, given the preponderant use of science and engineering, the IITs could be the campuses where such new life science technologies can be developed.

The route to such development lies in creating centres of excellence, for each of the solution areas that have been discussed in the foregoing in an illustrative manner. For example, there could be centres of excellence for cellular engineering, NIGA modelling, network rejuvenation, diagnostic efficiency, robotic surgery, bio-materials development, pharmaceutical discovery, and device optimization. These, and other similar centres, should be bound together by an integrated human life science technology system which understands the engineering of the human body and mind in a holistic manner.

As a fundamental requirement for the new stream of life science technologies, the current distinction between biological sciences oriented curricula and the mathematics oriented curricula (the former leading to medicine and the latter leading to engineering) needs to be done away with. Undergraduate students should be provided with equal grounding in physical sciences and biological sciences to be able to absorb the nuances of medicine and engineering effortlessly.

If the medical education as envisaged herein needs to take root in the IITs, the analytical capabilities need a significant leg-up. More powerful liquid and gas chromatography and mass spectroscopy instruments capable of not only conventional analytical research but also bio-analytical development and detection of entities in the minutest pico and ppq ranges would be required. Similarly, biological laboratories which can develop in vitro cellular models based on genetic sciences will also be required. New genetic engineering equipment such as protein extraction and purification equipment, gene sequences, microarrays will need to be installed. It is likely that upgradation of infrastructure alone would be in the order of one billion dollars for say five IITs together to start with.

Integrated life science technology programs at higher levels of education (post-graduation and research including doctoral and post-doctoral programs) must be flexible to accept entrants via basic bachelor's degree in engineering or medicine. Establishment of autonomous life science technology centres within the IITs with their own dedicated programs will see a new dream fulfilled in higher education scene in India. With such an effort, India could lead an educational revolution in life science technologies even on a global basis. Figure 3.2 summarises the actions for IITs in developing life science technologies.

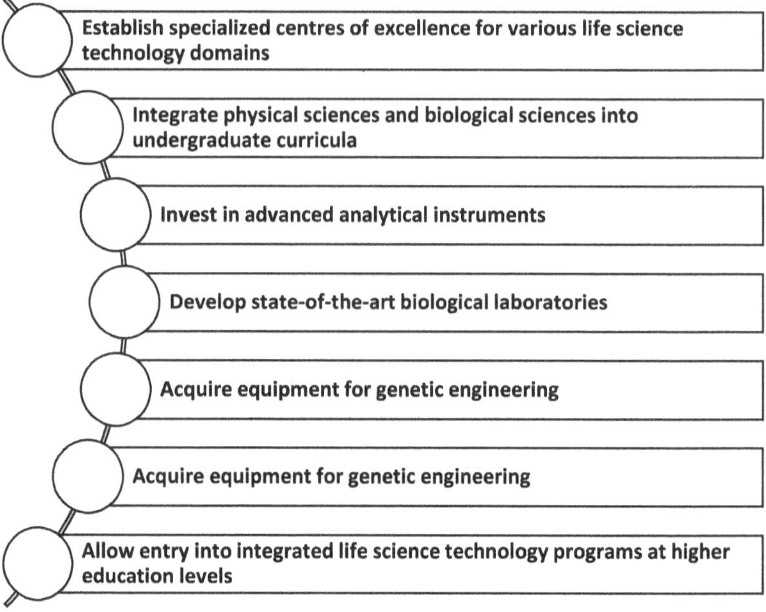

Figure 3.2: Actions for IITs in Developing Life Science Technologies

Science, Technology, Entrepreneurship, Management, and Studentship (STEMS)

The Five-Component Transformational Paradigm for India

A nation's competitive advantage is built by its scientific and technological innovation on one hand and its managerial and entrepreneurial ethic on the other. As India aspires to become the third largest economy in the globe, in an accelerated manner, by 2028, the above four factors, enhanced by the new graduate stock, would need to be the key drivers of the transformation. In the past, India has been losing its brightest scientists and engineers to greener pastures abroad. With India poised to become the third largest economy in the world, this trend should logically be reversed, with more overseas citizens contributing to the Indian economic transformation. More particularly, it will be the commitment of bright scientists and engineers of India to stay in India or return to India after their post-graduation and research studies abroad, that would make India an industrial and economic superpower. This would potentiate the managerial and entrepreneurial force in the economy. Figure 4.1 illustrates the key factors for competitive advantage to drive India's transformation.

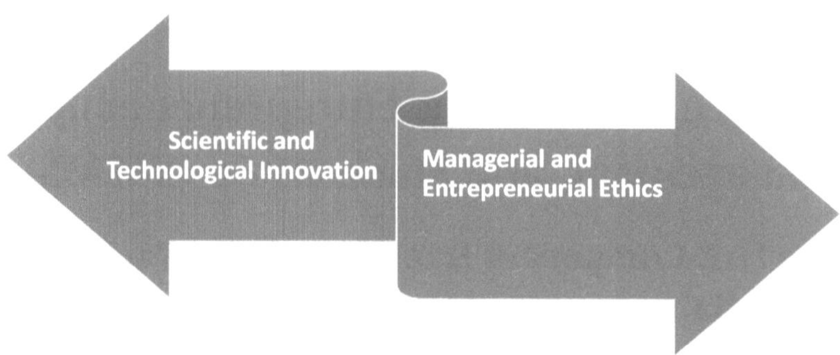

Figure 4.1: Driving India's Transformation: Key Factors for Competitive Advantage

India is no longer only the world's back-office. The country is fast moving into the arena of global manufacturing and design. In fact, smart science and frugal engineering are the new buzz words that are gaining acceptance as concepts that are typically Indian. The ability of the Indian scientists to invent new processes and discover new drug candidates at fractional time and cost has drawn the interest of global pharmaceutical industry. The ability of the country's engineers to design and establish projects in the shortest possible time with low investment costs and their creativity to design functional products with different value points is recognized globally. Scientists and engineers, therefore, have a great opportunity with the kind of transformation and expectation anchored around India.

Science and Technology

Science and technology (or engineering) are the twin pillars on which a nation's economic progress and social development are built. All the developed nations owe their progress to the fundamental contributions of their scientists and engineers whose inventions and discoveries led to creation of new product and business lines. Science is a systematic study of the behaviour of the physical world with discovery, theorization and experimentation constantly expanding the envelope of knowledge. Engineering is the domain of applying science to design, develop, build, and maintain equipment, facilities and infrastructure as well as operate production systems to deliver products and services. Both science and engineering are inspired by a spirit of enquiry, a philosophy of detail and an ethic of commitment. These great disciplines teach a student to be data based and yet innovative and creative. Emphasis on quality and safety are an integral part of science and technology.

Indian science and technology have traditionally focused on followership. While several institutions in new cutting-edge domains are set up and new projects of national importance taken up in India, results have been less than satisfactory due to non-fostering of a culture of innovation. The problem is accentuated by lack of funding and low compensation and incentive structures in the research field. Even institutes of national importance such as the Indian Institutes of Technology and Indian Institute of Science as well as laboratories of Council of Scientific and Industrial Research have not been able to come up with commercially viable patented new technologies. For example, according to statistics released by the World Intellectual Property Organization (WIPO), India filed in 2022 only 2,618 patent applications compared to China's 70,015. The good news, however, is that the infrastructure and talent pool for a greater intellectual thrust exists in India. The challenge is one of sparking the research interest with strategic direction, performance management and incentive development.

Entrepreneurship and management

Science and technology constitute the core of a nation, but entrepreneurship and management are the catalysts for application of science and technology for human endeavour. A great nation can be built only by entrepreneurship, which creates new lines of activity, new areas of business, new enterprises and even new industries based on entrepreneurial ideas and passion. Entrepreneurship is typically based on new, innovative products and services as well as processes, improved and more efficient manufacturing or novel and creative delivery of products and services to customers. Whatever be the domain of value chain which houses entrepreneurship, innovative use of science and technology lies at the core of entrepreneurship. The wide canvas where entrepreneurship can make its mark has no limits at all. Established and new product lines as well as sunset and sunrise product lines all qualify for entrepreneurial development. Often, the start-up entrepreneurial effort is individual or small group driven.

Management has long been realized as the interdisciplinary and interfaculty approach that applies and utilizes all forms of capital, human, machine and financial to generate value for the firms, investors, society and the nation through products and services. The growth and value creation of successful organizations, even of entrepreneurial organizations after their initial success, is clearly attributable to good management. The decline and value erosion of failed organizations is similarly attributable to bad management. While good management is a part of successful entrepreneurship, management, in one sense, takes over where entrepreneurship leaves: from initial local success to sustainable global scale-up and from the first specialization to eventual integration or diversification. One of the important tasks and great challenges of management is finding the right blend of technical and human factors. Successful management is also one of evolving its own model, contextually relevant to the company, society, and nation.

India's opportunities and challenges

India has tremendous strengths with its vast pool of scientists and technologists, and a fast developing managerial and entrepreneurial base ought to have been a major industrial and economic power by now. However, economic, and industrial policies of post-independence India, close to a very long period of 45 years between 1947 and 1992, followed a socialistic pattern. Most decisions to create capacity, whether in education or industry, were limited by resource availability rather than revenue generation and by demand control rather than market expansion. While a great measure of self-reliance, economic independence and scientific and technological maturity was achieved as a result, India lagged in economic and innovation indices. The initial stirrings became evident from the 1980s when Indian industrialists began to become externally oriented and from the 1990s when the government embarked upon economic liberalization. The economic growth rate has in the past few years has moved up to 6-8 percent per annum, from the previous historical long term, multi-decade average of 4.5 percent.

While there has been a quantitative expansion of capacities in India, post-liberalization, with a flood of new products and services, from automobiles to aircraft and from flat panel televisions to cellular phones, most of it is consumption driven. The internal processors and operating systems of most products and the smarter of the new products in totality are still based on imports from more advanced nations. The Indian automobile industry may have absorbed the imported product technologies and manufacturing processes but most of the sophisticated equipment from machining centres to robotic welders as well as precision measuring instruments are still imported. The Indian pharmaceutical industry could be the largest exporter of medicines to the most advanced countries, but the laboratory and manufacturing equipment are of imported pedigree in such lines. India excels in software but has not yet produced a search engine or social network. Science, technology, entrepreneurship and management have to share equal responsibility for the current state of sub-optimization of India's potential.

Back to basics, a leap into future

India's IT and manufacturing outsourcing consumption would sustain a consumption driven market expansion and entry of several new products which are largely indigenously manufactured, and assembled through completely knocked down

(CKD) and semi knocked down (SKD) routes and in some cases even as imported completely built units (CBU). However, India as the world's third largest economy cannot afford to rest with a linear scale-up of current capabilities and approaches. There is a need for transformational shift. As illustrated in Figure 4.2, this shift must have two approaches. The first relates to a focus on fundamentals in science and technology and the second relates to a qualitative boost to the Indian managerial and entrepreneurial capabilities. Government of India, in recent years, has taken specific steps to achieve a transformation in Indian innovation, manufacturing, and entrepreneurship through technology-oriented investment policies.

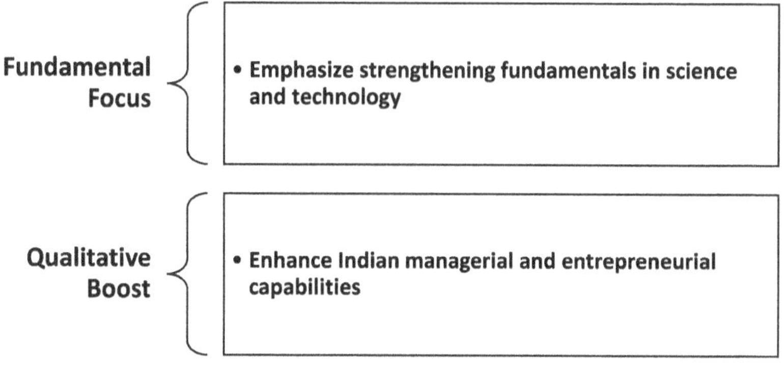

Figure 4.2: Two Strategic Approaches for India's Transformation

Scientists and technologists of India need to direct a portion of their intellectual efforts to drive fundamental innovations. One model could be to differentiate between organizations dedicated to fundamental innovation and those focused on followership or application of innovation. This is best accomplished in certain established industries such as pharmaceuticals as well as in multiple sunrise industries. Most industries require co-development of fundamental innovation and applied innovation. For example, it would be impractical for an architectural firm to design only green and novel buildings or for an automobile firm to manufacture only autonomous cars. Commencing fundamental innovations in niche areas and mass customizing them is a challenge for scientists, technologists, managers, and entrepreneurs.

Factor combination

Any level of science and technology planning cannot be actualized without matching resources. There could be three ways to support this endeavour, one through wholly public investments, second through wholly private investments and the third through public-private partnerships. The aggregate investment on fundamental research should be at least 10 percent of gross domestic product, whether coming through public, private or joint methodologies. As one is aware, innovation-led global companies devote 15 to 20 percent of their turnover to research and development. Governments and industry associations need to chalk out a strategic plan for fundamental research as guidance for the industry and governments.

Similarly, there must be a focus on the fundamentals of robust management and creative entrepreneurship. Indian management has of late been gaining international recognition for its end-to-end conceptualization, risk-integrated decision making, creative multitasking, and speedy execution. The model, however, needs to be more deepened and broad-based to cover every enterprise and agency. Management institutions would need to take the lead by dedicating at least one semester of the typical two-year management courses to Indian management. It is time that Indian management is translated from an abstract approach realized by only a few to a tangible construct accessible to all.

And most certainly, entrepreneurship needs a major boost to support the transformation of the Indian industry and economy. Entrepreneurship could occur at any level and at any age. While young graduates are often encouraged to become entrepreneurs rather than job seekers the whole employment and retirement system should have the flexibility and fluidity to encourage entrepreneurship at any point of time in one's career, including post-retirement. For example, working managers and leaders could be encouraged to take up parts of industrial value chain as entrepreneurial ventures. Corporate entities need to establish entrepreneurship endowment funds and corpuses to support such entrepreneurial forays. Yet another mode could be to offer additional retirement funds to high performance executives linked solely to their commitment to set up entrepreneurial firms.

From 'STEM' to 'STEMS'

Clearly, Science, Technology, Entrepreneurship and Management (STEM) model is the foundation of a nation's economic and industrial progress. India, however, has as its forte a fifth dimension as it seeks to be transformative over the next 25 years. This relates to India's very young demographic profile (30 percent of population aged below 15 years) and the vast educational infrastructure that could be quantitatively and qualitatively expanded. While the early Indian governments laid the foundations of a highly capacity regulated higher educational system, entry of private sector into the engineering and science college system from the 1980s has revolutionized the education scenario in terms of quantitative easing.

India has presently a uniquely large educational base out of Tier 1 and Tier 2 cities, which needs to be upgraded and diversified into rural satellite centres. Despite a relatively low overall literacy score at primary level (which itself needs further improvement from the current 77.7 percent), India has one of the largest talent pools in the world, which needs to be leveraged more fully. India has, for example, more than 95 lakh graduates passing out every year, of which more than 20.5 lakh are science and mathematics graduates, 12 lakhs are post-graduates, and 8 lakhs are engineers. India with its vast network of over 1,113 universities, 43,796 colleges and 11,296 standalone institutions has contributed to the development of the second largest pool of scientists and engineers (31.7% of the world's total STEM graduates) in the world.

As students are taught to become scientists, engineers and managers, the right experiential learning structures and inputs on creativity, innovation, management and entrepreneurship would build capabilities and confidence in them to take up entrepreneurship. If even 10 percent of the scientists and engineers graduating each year in India choose to become entrepreneurs with unique ideas in the chosen field, the student force would be really transforming India. This is not to say that entrepreneurship is the only route to fulfilment of a larger purpose in life. The key here is being entrepreneurial. Whatever the avocation chosen by a student, whether as a laboratory scientist, shop floor engineer, product developer, information technologist or even a business analyst, the focus should be on being entrepreneurial in thinking and execution.

For student entrepreneurship to succeed, research and manufacturing establishments as well as businesses must be more open to accepting and trusting students as interns and providing them with challenging projects of long duration rather than paper studies of short duration. The highly successful model of medical internship must be made mandatory in engineering education as well, with industries required to take on board students as co-workers with or understudies to scientists, technologists, and managers. This will strengthen the ability of students to cope with real world industrial complexities. When this happens, STEMS – the science, technology, entrepreneurship, management, and studentship framework – would be a well-balanced five component transformative model for India.

STEMS as a collaborative paradigm

Today's globalized world is highly competitive. India, with the global attention and adulation it is receiving, is on the path to attain the super economic power status. The good news is that a fast-growing market and a highly youthful society are geared to make the transformation happen. India needs to innovate for its own new products and services, besides constantly enhancing the value of all current products and services. India should lead the world in upholding quality, protecting safety, reducing costs, and eliminating waste. At the same time, once in few years Indian industry and business will have to reinvent themselves with completely new ways of doing things to achieve new levels in global competitiveness.

Such a transformative journey cannot happen by the individual efforts of scientists, technologists, managers, or entrepreneurs. India needs to move towards an ideal national system of mutually collaborative science, technology, entrepreneurship, and management, each of them progressing with vertical and horizontal linkages, all the way from student days, and in a strategic framework. For example, in a strategic framework, innovations in material sciences that lead to better engineering of components, better designs of equipment and tooling that lead to better components from designs, component changes that drive model makeovers must be holistically integrated. Enterprises and entrepreneurs must lead such transformative inflexions in science, technology, and management on a continuous basis. From the current diffused and random resort to science, technology, entrepreneurship and management, a more holistic and integrated emphasis on the five-component model is required. This will require development and execution of a great new educational and application strategy of science, technology, entrepreneurship, and management to reinforce India in its transformative journey as an economic superpower.

Chapter 5

Government-Academy-Industry-Networking (GAIN)

A Paradigm for Indian National Innovation

The foundations of India as a knowledge society lie in our colleges and universities. The society would not be intellectually what it is but for the educational institutions which transform human beings into human resources. Similarly, the foundations of an economic society lie in the industries and businesses. The society would not be economically what it is today but for the industries and businesses that not only utilize the human intellectual capital developed but also generate new knowledge to achieve commercial results. Despite this intrinsic synergy, it is of concern that industry (which includes business and administration) and academics (which covers educational institutions) tend to be quite detached from each other. The Government of India's New Education Policy which promotes diversification of education, with a bias towards vocational development should make a difference in this context.

Amongst all fields of knowledge generation in academia and knowledge application in industry, science and technology emerge as the primary drivers of development, requiring the highest levels of teaching, research, industrial development, investment, and commercialization. These two fields are also the fields that require constant experimentation and research to develop new bodies of knowledge that can be commercially utilized anew. Science and technology are thus not only essential for social and economic development but also constitute the twin areas in which both the industry and academia have an enormous stake. Science, technology, industry, and academy thus constitute the four essentials of national development and global competitiveness. The greater the collaboration amongst the industry and academics the greater would be the benefit for the nation in terms of the amazing results of science and technology.

Common and uncommon

Whenever two entities have goals that apparently converge but have strategies that diverge, there could be certain basic differences affecting the combined system. In the modern world, academics are the engine of economic development through innovation, in addition to the established role of social development through education. Similarly, industry is expected to be a responsible citizen in addition to the role of efficient wealth maximiser. However, the routes taken by the industry and academics are traditionally, and even now, seem to be different. Academics see their deliverables in terms of people and qualifications while industry sees its deliverables in terms of products and services. The factor of people, and more fundamentally of knowledge and talent, which constitutes the output of the academic system, and the input of the industrial system is not utilized the best way.

Similarly, the disparities are also more apparent than real. Industry believes that its core requirement is speed of execution, and that the academic environment is not exactly speed or delivery oriented. On the contrary, it is perhaps the educational system that has a very rigorous and time bound study calendar which it implements with predetermined accuracy. Academics believe that industrialists are content with application and repeatability for most part and that they are less concerned about knowledge and creativity as a work ethic. On the contrary, it is perhaps more incumbent than ever for the industries to be creative to retain or achieve competitiveness.

Drug discovery as a case study

While the concept of academic and industry collaboration is applicable for all industries, the pharmaceutical industry has the promise to be a major domain for such collaboration. The Big Pharmaceutical Corporations that are traditionally dedicated to innovative drug discovery have moved away from a "high cost, long lead, low productivity" model of conducting all research in-house to a "low cost, low lead, smart development" model of industrial outsourcing and academic collaboration. Academic institutions abroad play a major role in triggering new scientific and technological development through academic research and converting them into industrial activity and business wealth. Genentech is a great example of this process. Many drugs that have been discovered or are in the development pipeline owe their origins to academic research. Some examples include Pemetrexed (Alimta), Darunavir (Prezista), Astrasentan (Xinlay) and Emtricitabine (Emtriva).

According to GlobalData's Looking Ahead to 2023 – the Future of Pharma report, the top five drug launches are predominantly dominated by large-cap American pharmaceutical companies, making up 80 percent of the representation. It is not surprising that the United States maintains a dominant position in the launch of blockbuster drugs. This is due to its role as the global leader in per capita spending on prescription drugs, contributing to about 30 to 40 percent of the global pharmaceutical market. On certain other criteria such as share in discovering drugs for unmet medical needs and drugs for orphan needs, biotech and universities had a higher share. Willingness and creativity to experiment, which is a true benchmark of accomplished academia could be a driver for this. Quite apart from discovery of drugs, academic and industrial sponsors can collaborate on drug structure prospecting studies, receptor identification, biomarker development, mechanism of action studies, molecular pharmacology, molecular biology, target development, new dosage forms and novel drug delivery technologies.

Creativity and serendipity

Creativity has no boundaries. It is interesting that many of the blockbuster drugs approved in Japan were discovered by non-pharmaceutical corporations. In fact, it is a uniquely Japanese phenomenon to have pharmaceutical operations within non-pharmaceutical companies in Japan. Evoxac (cervimiline hydrochloride, partly by Snow Brand), Starlix (nateglenide, Ajinomoto) and Spectracef (cefditorin pivoxil, Meiji Seika) are the three Japanese drugs discovered by food companies. Eloxatin (oxaliplatin) came from a precious metals company, Tanaka Kikinzoku Kogyo. Several agricultural and plant products have given rise to medicinal products and food supplements. The willingness to constantly search for new applications has helped scientists to be creative.

Serendipity is one of the many factors that contribute to drug discovery. It has played a role in the discovery of prototype psychotropic drugs that led to modern pharmacological treatment in psychiatry. It has also played a role in the discovery of several drugs that have had an impact on the development of cardiovascular drugs. Serendipity in drug discovery implies the finding of one thing while looking for something else. This was the case in six serendipitous discoveries (out of a basket of twelve drugs covered in a Vanderbilt University research; Dialogues Clinical Neurosciences, 2006: 8(3): 335-44) namely, aniline purple, penicillin, lysergic acid diethylamide, meprobamate, chlorpromazine, and imipramine. In the case of three drugs, i.e., potassium bromide, chloral hydrate, and lithium, the discovery was serendipitous because an utterly false rationale led to correct empirical results; and in case of two others, i.e., iproniazid and sildenafil, because valuable indications were found for these drugs which were not initially those sought. The discovery of one of the twelve drugs, chlordiazepoxide, was sheer luck.

The freedom of academics sparks the creativity of science and helps cross-functional and cross-domain discoveries.

Breakthrough concepts of artificial intelligence and biological cloning have resulted from the works of university professors and researchers. Most Nobel prizes in science and medicine are garnered by university academics. Great institutions like Karolinska University are not only in the forefront of education and research but also in the vanguard of an intellectual ecosystem for entrepreneurship and commercial development. Many of the Silicon Valley startups have university connections that enable great new ideas of professors and researchers who take up commercialization of innovations as entrepreneurial ventures. There is no reason why the Indian Institutes of Technology (IITs), the Indian Institute of Science (IISc), National Institutes of Technology (NIT) and other premier universities cannot create globally competitive knowledge ecosystems in India.

Figure 5.1 shows the difference between creativity and serendipity.

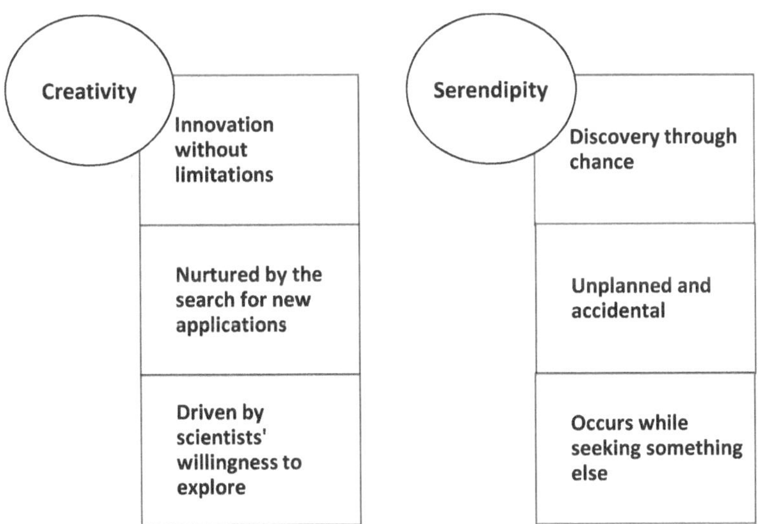

Figure 5.1: Difference Between Creativity and Serendipity

Competency building

In parallel to the product-focused research, academic institutions and industrial organizations can collaborate to develop students with skills and competencies that are required for cutting edge science and technology and convert the skills into commercial capabilities. The world is placing significant hope and trust on India delivering the unique advantages of frugal engineering, novel technologies, high quality, rapid commercialization, and cost-competitiveness. This requires a talent pool which has not only an excellent knowledge base but also an ability to apply such knowledge to industrial scale development and global networking. The relative shortage of such talent, despite the high number of graduates, postgraduates and researchers has resulted in a skew in the employment market. Companies and educational institutions must collaborate to develop the requisite talent pool. Two-way sabbaticals of industry professionals and academic professors, mutual lecture sessions, live projects in industries, symposia, and consulting assignments by universities would be great ways to strengthen the talent pool.

Institutions of higher learning and innovation not only provide the private sector with skilled human resources, but also support the sector in many other ways, including research and development. Collaboration between the academia and industry plays a crucial role in fostering public and private sector competitiveness, through both indirect and direct knowledge transfer. The indirect knowledge transfer is achieved through such activities as industrial training, using members of the academia as consultants in the private sector, holding joint workshops and conferences, and journal publications. On the other hand, direct knowledge transfer is achieved through collaborative research and/or purchases of patents. It should be noted that in both types of knowledge transfer, knowledge flow is in both directions, between academia and industry. Knowledge from the academia to the industry is used to improve products and services, while the knowledge from industry to the academia is used to define disciplines, develop curricula, design short courses, and improve pedagogy.

Government, the vertex of knowledge triangle

Globally, governments have played a significant role in fostering industry academic collaboration either by policy or financial incentives. The progress made by several developed economies is directly attributable to the knowledge and talent ecosystems that governments, universities, and industries built together. The United States has been the pioneer in funding academic research and institutional development of knowledge with commercialization of intellectual property. Europe has been also a major harbinger of scientific and technological innovation for commercialization. A study of select Asian countries by the World Intellectual Property Organization (WIPO) as reflected in its work "Technology Transfer, Intellectual Property and Effective University-Industry Partnerships: The Experience of China, India, Japan, Philippines, The Republic of Korea, Singapore and Thailand (2007)" has interesting insights.

In these countries, development and expansion of University-Industry (U-I) relationships during the study decade had been a result of goal-oriented and deliberate public policy efforts. The areas of focus included: defining the legal status of universities and their professors, relaxing or removing regulations that prevented faculty members from working with companies, developing policies on intellectual property rights, establishing technology transfer offices, creating funding schemes, and ensuring adequate financial resources for research and development activities at universities. Asian countries, both developed and developing, demonstrated a consensus that universities and public laboratories should make greater contributions to countries' overall economic growth and competitiveness. While universities, industries, and publicly funded research institutions should be allowed to develop working relations with each other through their own initiative, governments also have a responsibility to establish laws and practices that would give proper incentives towards collaborative research activities. At the same time, WIPO cautions that we must be careful not to forget the importance of long-term scientific goals and educational responsibility. Universities should not cave into the pressure to generate quick commercial outcomes.

In all the Asian countries that participated in the WIPO project, some type of policy framework, underpinned by laws and government regulations, has been put in place over the previous two decades. As illustrated in Figure 5.2, according to WIPO, ideally, the policy framework should serve three purposes: first, to state publicly the intention of the government with respect to the direction universities and industry should take; second, to lay down legal rules for the conduct of universities and industry, for example in relation to the management of IPRs; and third, to secure financial resources and incentives to facilitate collaboration. Not all countries have policy frameworks that serve all the three purposes. In certain countries, the legal status of universities needed to be redefined by new laws so that they could operate as independent and responsible entities. In others, there was no need for new legislation. In some countries, governments are taking pro-active measures to boost U-I collaboration, while in other countries they play more backseat roles, allowing universities and industries to determine their own courses of action. The legal frameworks are very different among the Asian countries that participated in this project. In addition to the legal framework, some countries draw up basic plans and goals for U-I collaboration with a view to setting forth future directions and accelerating the trend. Such basic plans are meant to be reviewed and if necessary, modified regularly to consider the progress to date.

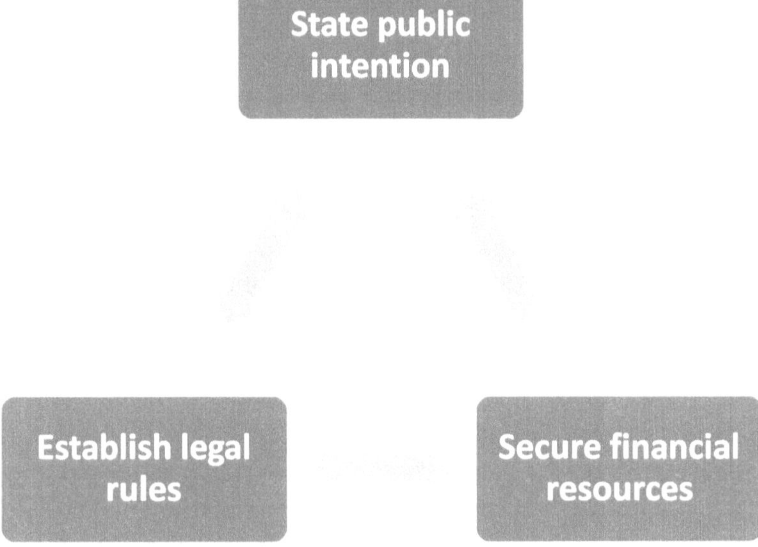

Figure 5.2: WIPO's Key Policy Framework Objectives

'GAIN' as a paradigm for India

In India, which has some of the better recognized university, industrial and legal systems of the world, the Government has a major role to play in the academy-industry collaboration. For one, most high level scientific and technological institutions in India are sponsored, funded, or regulated by the government. Secondly, government funding and tax policies have a major role to play in seeding the thoughts of collaboration and incentivizing. In the US as well, federal funding is a major trigger for academic research. In India, the Department of Scientific and Industrial Research (DSIR) of the Government plays a major catalytic role through programs such as Industrial R&D Promotion Program, Technology Development and Demonstration Program, Technopreneur Promotion Program and Technology Development and Utilization Program. Of these, TDDP has been playing a significant role in strengthening the interface between industry R&D establishments and academic institutions through a variety of schemes and projects. Yet, the impact in terms of intellectual property creation and commercialization is not as deep as it ought to be.

Eventually, for a national impact, India would need a model of Government-Academy-Industry-Networking that is win-win for all the stake holders and the nation at large. One of the concerns the industry has in sponsored research is the protection of intellectual property while the academia similarly has the concern for creative freedom. There is a need to combine creativity and novelty of positive university thinking with the rigour and discipline of real proof-of-concept that is required by the industry and regulators to achieve win-win commercialization. In this joint endeavour there is no question of who is better; chemistry is as important as biology, and extending it further, discovery of a preliminary proof-of-concept drug and its advancement to commercialization are equally important. Government on its part would like the educational institutions to generate some royalties out of the intellectual property generated which would help the institutions reinvest for better infrastructure.

Under the GAIN paradigm, the government would develop, through a joint expert committee, a standardized and transparent model of academy-industry collaborative agreements which will enable open collaboration and cross-fertilization. In certain sunrise sectors, the government would need to take specific initiatives. For example, the Taiwanese government launched a Project called "Two Trillions & Two Stars" to promote industry development, in which the two stars referred to the semiconductor and display industries. To convert the traditional production-strength business model into advanced technology, the need of qualified talents was identified by Taiwan as a crucial factor to keep up with the future. Therefore, Government, Industry, Academy and Research Institutes cooperated to provide technology training programs in Taiwan. One action initiated by Industrial Development Bureau, Minister of Economic Affairs (MOEA) was to establish "Semiconductor Institute" in 2003 to meet the challenge of professional and technical talents shortage issue. In addition, different kinds of organizations worked together to synergize programs for international investment and local industries.

Government of India has now taken up the development of world-class semiconductor industry in India as a strategic goal. This augurs very well. Apart from investments by Indian and global firms, India's several thousand colleges and universities as well as hundreds of public and private research laboratories could be catalysed into a knowledge network for all the industries by government policies. Transfer of academic research to entrepreneurial ventures on zero fee but commercialization linked royalties would be a great way to develop faith in the accomplishments of Indian research that are dormant. Larger firms and universities can play a more proactive role by setting up cutting edge centres of excellence in sunrise fields. Government can extend its effective role by providing the seed capital for such ventures which usually require mega capital. Active participation by the institutions and industries for such centres would be enabled if the sponsoring units are provided dedicated access to facilities and research. Centres for biotechnology, nanotechnology, semiconductors, artificial intelligence, genetics, and alternate energy are best supported by such collaborative endeavours.

Knowledge cities for GAIN

The Government of India announced a National Manufacturing Policy which envisages the creation of 12 mega National Investment and Manufacturing Zones (NIMZs) in the country to spur massive industrialization and make Manufacturing contribute to 25 percent of the GDP. For achieving global competitiveness and self-sufficiency through manufacturing, knowledge that can stimulate product and process competitiveness is even more necessary. GoI should consider the IITs, the IISc, the NITs and CSIR laboratories as well as the GoI recognized industrial R&D centres (totalling say 100 to start with) to take the lead for creating the knowledge cities around them. Networking would be as important as physical assets to translate GAIN into a successful operating paradigm. As with National Manufacturing Policy, GoI should suggest a National Knowledge Policy, with National Knowledge Cities and Government-Academy-Industry-Networking as its principal platforms, and national innovation and global competitiveness as the principal objectives.

Chapter 6

Indian Mission for Artificial Intelligence Networking (IMAIN)

A Futuristic Paradigm for Progressive Healthcare

The paradigm of human healthcare could undergo a dramatic transformation in the years and the decades to come. Toyota Motor Corporation (Toyota), the world leader in automobiles, unveiled robots and robotic devices that assist elderly and disabled people perform day to day activities. Previously unthinkable tasks such as climbing the stairs by aged people with knee immobility or getting out of bed for bedridden people could be soon a matter of realization rather than hope. Toyota is confident that these new robotic developments are not going to be mere technological showpieces but would be smart companions, commercially available. This marks a new height scaled by engineering which consistently has been crossing new milestones in diagnostics and minimally invasive and non-invasive surgeries (the latest ones being the ultra-precision scanners, directed radio knife for oncology and ultrasound surgery for uterine fibroids). One may imagine that engineering strides would continue to lead to unforeseen improvements in the lives of patients and the needy.

At the other end, research into regenerative medicine continues to make steady progress. Regenerative medicine is the process of replacing or regenerating human cells, tissues, or organs to restore or establish normal function. This field holds the promise of regenerating damaged tissues and organs in the body by replacing damaged tissue and/or by stimulating the body's own repair mechanisms to heal previously irreparable tissues or organs. Regenerative medicine also empowers scientists to grow tissues and organs in the laboratory and safely implant them when the body cannot heal itself. Because a person's own (autologous) cord blood stem cells can be safely infused back into that individual without being rejected by the body's immune system — and because they have unique characteristics compared to other sources of stem cells — they are an increasing focus of regenerative medicine research.

Indian medicine, regenerative potential

India has the doctors' hands that cure like the best from anywhere else in the world. Indian doctors have also demonstrated the ability to utilize the best of scanning and surgical devices to enhance the efficacy and certainty of surgeries. There is a view that the Indian hospital infrastructure is so grossly inadequate, and the availability of doctors and beds is so woefully low that it makes little sense to focus on the futuristic areas of medicine. While there is an element of truth in this, every inflexion of technology offers the opportunity for developing and emerging countries such as India to leapfrog into cutting edge technologies. There are nearly thirty institutes in India such as L V Prasad Eye Institute and Sankara Nethralaya which are conducting successful research in the use of stem cells for various degenerative diseases. Given India's population spread, disease burden and medical expertise, regenerative medicine could be a great new area of research and application for healthcare in India.

Importantly, regenerative medicine has the potential to solve the problem of the shortage of organs available for donation compared to the number of patients that require life-saving organ transplantation. It will also solve the problem of organ transplant rejection since the organ's cells will match that of the patient. The use of cord blood stem cells in treating conditions such as brain injury, cardio-vascular ailments, Type 1 diabetes, stroke, eye repair and hearing restoration would grow in future. As several clinical and pre-clinical studies currently underway demonstrate, cord blood stem cells will likely be an important resource as medicine advances towards harnessing the body's own cells for treatment. The field of regenerative medicine can be expected to benefit greatly as additional cord blood stem cell applications are researched and more people have access to their own preserved cord blood. Figure 6.1 shows the advantages of Regenerative medicine.

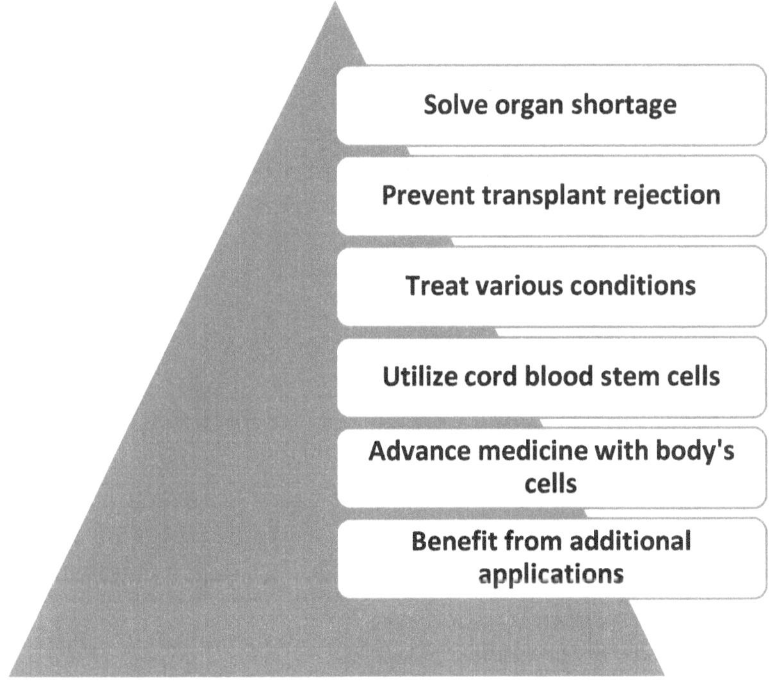

Figure 6.1: Advantages of Regenerative Medicine

Indian technology, mechanical advantage

At first glance, India could be perceived as a nation that has to be dependent on imported medical technology for perpetuity. However, Indian technology has also its pluses, especially in mechanical, metallurgical, machine tool, automobile, component, and aerospace domains. With the machining and casting precision levels having gone up to exacting standards more recently, the next horizon of precision tooling and die technologies, and mastering component level precision is not an insurmountable goal for the Indian industry. With its Jaipur foot, India has shown that it can provide low-cost solutions for enhancing patient mobility. There is, therefore, significant scope for the Indian industry to participate in the healthcare robotics revolution. What India needs is the semiconductor and micro-electronics technology-set which can be supplemented by the software technology skill sets that would be extensively required in robots and robotic devices.

The Indian private and public sector corporations to date have focused only on basic and consumer industries. The aspiration to engage themselves in newly developing technologies has been somewhat on a low key. This is demonstrated by the reluctance to develop high-end products (for example, luxury cars, precision forgings or cold rolled steel) even in the industries where Indian corporations are strong. However, of late there has been a clear glimmer of hope. Tata Motors' turnaround of Land Rover Jaguar and development of new high-end models with Indian components indicates that Indian industry could secure a niche in complex engineering if it sets it heart on the goal. This would, however, require large conglomerates and government corporations to dedicate certain portion of their research and manufacturing expenditure to high technology products.

Artificial intelligence, natural competency

India would have a natural, national advantage in developing products of artificial intelligence, an essential facet of robotics. Robotic devices help patients who have some level of mental ability to understand how to overcome physical disability with robotic assistance. Often, seriously ill patients would require caretakers to help them take robotic assistance. Artificial intelligence would be one technology that could help patients comprehend their needs and cope with their disabilities, and enable doctors, nurses and caretakers fulfil their responsibilities more efficiently and accurately. Artificial intelligence is more than a computer providing a set of programmed instructions or a series of question-and-answer sessions. Artificial intelligence that is relevant to the healthcare sector requires real time analysis of the patient's faculties and comparing them with what should have been a healthy person's faculties and guiding the patients as well as the robots through the gap bridging.

Artificial intelligence would be helpful to the larger universe of doctors, nurses, and caretakers as well. Artificial intelligence would also vary in its scope and application based on the disease state of the patient. A patient affected by Parkinson's disease would have needs that are different from those of a patient affected by epilepsy, for example. The deficit in faculties varies significantly across disease states. Artificial intelligence could also provide significant reinforcement to devices that are implanted in a patient to regulate his or her physiological state such as a cardiac pacemaker or a diabetic insulin pump. Sensory technologies play a major role in developing a patient baseline and a target health line for artificial intelligence. Given the billions of information bytes and logic sets that would need to be captured and codified even in a modest project of artificial intelligence, the Indian information technology industry could play a major role.

Multiple disciplines, singular focus

From complex mathematics and sophisticated engineering to involved psychology and intricate neurology, virtually every discipline is required to develop a viable platform of artificial intelligence. Unlike any other discipline, artificial intelligence has no unifying theory. No direct correlations and influences are possible either. Human biology would be quite relevant to healthcare artificial intelligence. Amongst all diverse approaches developed for artificial intelligence, from programmed logic to random simulation, mathematics, and statistics with integration of neurological science and human behavioural logic provide a useful approach. Developers are now seized of the methodologies and tools that could add even empathy and emotion to artificial intelligence to mimic human intelligence and behaviour as much as possible.

A major challenge in artificial intelligence relates to storage and computing power as well as energy consumption. This is being addressed by the various stakeholders; even otherwise the computing power of computers would continue to grow exponentially. What could limit artificial intelligence is the sheer plurality of behaviour of human mind. Even billions of codes could prove unequal to the individual shades of variation in human behaviour. It is, therefore, necessary that while deploying as many disciplines as possible to develop viable platforms of artificial intelligence, developers should go deep into specific fields. For example, initial focus could be on disease conditions which have faculty deficit rather than total faculty absence. As the discipline of artificial intelligence proves itself, it becomes easier to integrate the learning into newer devices for more complex diseases such as stroke and Alzheimer's disease.

Indian potential, capable entities

India has probably several advantages to become a centre of global excellence for artificial intelligence. India traditionally has had one of the strongest bases for mathematics and statistics, which is now fortified with multiple disciplines of engineering, especially software engineering. The strategy to become a global power in artificial intelligence has four components for India. The first is the building of supercomputers that can process billions of calculations and algorithms. The second is the multi-disciplinary programming effort required to create the artificial intelligence. The third is to integrate artificial intelligence with a host of advanced diagnostic and surgical devices to enhance the capabilities of physicians and surgeons. The fourth is to establish an optimal interface and governance between the patient, doctor, nurse, hospital, and caretakers. In each of the four areas India must take up visionary research and development.

India has demonstrated its capability to build supercomputers. As Japan's latest supercomputer developments indicate, there exist no limits for computing capability. To succeed in the domain of healthcare artificial intelligence, however, India will need to take the supercomputing revolution to the desktop and mobile computer fields, besides networking the central supercomputer to a host of servers. With reference to the multi-disciplinary programming, there are several institutes in India that are dedicated to advanced mathematics, computer sciences, biological sciences, and medical engineering as well as medical institutions dedicated to certain disease streams. These institutions can collaborate to develop the thinking and execution for artificial intelligence.

The networking of the above two capabilities with medical diagnostic and surgical hardware would be challenging given the fact that all such equipment is produced only by a few global leaders in medical technologies located in the developed world. That said, GE has been a pioneer in trying to explore the Indian advantage in developing new medical devices in India. India would need to create a value proposition for such equipment majors as the preferred partner for artificial intelligence. Despite the tremendous progress made in imaging of the body, interpretation of the results continues to be human dominated. In today's busy medical world, the doctor devotes very little time to analyse the hundreds of images taken per patient. Artificial intelligence can help the doctors extract the full value of the sophisticated imaging for achieving precision cures. This leads to the next step of limiting cure to the extent required, selectively and precisely, again with the help of artificial intelligence. Figure 6.2 shows the India's potential in artificial intelligence.

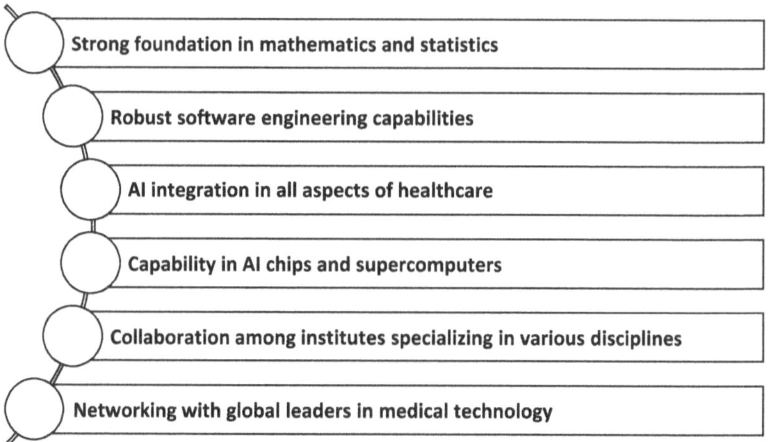

Figure 6.2: India's Potential in Artificial Intelligence

Palm reading, body scanning

Several pieces of mythology and fiction have come true in real life over the last several decades and centuries. A dramatically transformed healthcare scenario where science and technology deliver regenerative, reconstructive, and reinforcing options for human life would also come true one day. The world over, and across civilizations, palm reading has been popular to understand what the future foretells in terms of health and longevity, among others. In future, hopefully, body scanning backed by artificial intelligence would be, as easy and commonplace as palm reading, and would be a far better predictor of longevity and health. This enhanced predictive capability coupled with robotics and regeneration would make the world a better place to live and enjoy life, for sure.

In terms of developing a total healthcare ecosystem, comprising the patients, doctors, nurses, caretakers, and hospitals, based on equipment integrated with artificial intelligence, India can create a model of futuristic healthcare. Today's poor healthcare services need not deter India from taking a giant leap into this domain. It would be appropriate for the Government of India to develop a nationally networked program of artificial intelligence for specific diseases as a national technology mission. These need to be centrally funded as immediate commercial returns are difficult to envisage. India has some of the best leadership brains that are being utilized in conventional areas such as aerospace, defence, atomic energy, and unique individual identification number as well as in various medical, scientific, and engineering disciplines. Some of these leaders can be brought together to kick-start the Indian Mission for Artificial Intelligence Networking (IMAIN) for a new era of more assured healthcare.

Chapter 7

Foreign Educational Institutions in India

Right Priorities and Relevant Pathways

Globalisation of education can occur in three ways (Figure 7.1 illustrates). Firstly, Indian institutions, on their own, can qualify as top-class educational institutions globally through QS type of rankings. Secondly, Indian institutions can set up campuses abroad, by themselves or in collaboration with foreign institutions. Thirdly, foreign educational institutions can be allowed to set up bases in India, by themselves or in collaboration with Indian institutions. Some experts feel that these approaches lead to an unnecessary cost-push, given that the Indian educational system has reached a state of maturity and achieved global recognition. The proponents feel that the move is a logical extension of globalization with Indian universities being allowed to set up shops in foreign shores and vice versa. It is also hoped that foreign universities bring in the required investments for world-class educational experience in India. Some experiments of liberalization in India have had unwelcome fallouts of mass entry, leading to fragmented industry structures with low viability; some caution, therefore, is probably well merited.

Figure 7.1: Globalization of Education: Three Approaches

Foreign educational institutions in India

In the last decade, higher educational institutions (HEIs) have proliferated in India, but the educational scene has not improved correspondingly. India has 1,113 higher education institutions catering to 4.14 crore students, according to the Ministry of Education. The Universities Grants Commission (UGC) has established regulations for Higher Educational Institutions (HEIs) to collaborate with foreign universities on twinning, joint degrees, and dual degree programs. The Joint Degree program's curriculum will be created collaboratively by both partnering HEIs, and the certificate will be awarded by both Indian and foreign universities. To be eligible, students must complete at least 30 percent of their credits at each university.

Currently, 230 Indian HEIs and 1,256 foreign HEIs satisfy the eligibility criteria for the regulations. The Foreign Educational Institutions (Regulation of Entry and Operations Bill) 2010 did not receive sufficient support in Parliament and lapsed after the UPA government completed its term.

The Indian government aims to increase the Gross Enrolment Ratio (GER) in higher education from 27.1 percent in 2019-20 to 50 percent by 2035. Despite improvements in higher education, with 41 Indian HEIs in the QS World University Rankings 2023 and around 75 HEIs in the Times Higher Education World University Rankings 2023, Indian HEIs have yet to make it to the top 100s of these global rankings. Though not directly related, many students opt to study abroad for higher degrees, and government data shows that over 1.5 million Indian students went overseas for higher education (as of January 2023), with the aspiration of eventual employment there.

UGC rules

In 2023, The University Grants Commission (UGC) in India proposed draft rules for foreign universities interested in setting up campuses in the country. The rules permit freedom over fees and repatriation of funds abroad, and include special dispensation on regulatory, governance, and content norms in line with what is available to autonomous institutions in India. Foreign universities must rank among the top 500 internationally and will be subject to regulation by the UGC. These rules aim to address issues that had previously caused efforts to attract foreign universities to run aground. As per the data presented in Parliament, around 650,000 Indians enrolled in foreign universities in 2022, seeking superior education and entrepreneurial learning opportunities. This led to a substantial outflow of more than Rs 1,300 crore to fund their education. The University Grants Commission (UGC) plans to focus on these students and aims to draw international students to study in India.

UGC will form a permanent committee to review issues related to establishing and operating foreign higher educational institutions (FHEIs) in India. This committee will evaluate each application based on various factors, including the reputation of the educational institution, the academic programs they plan to offer, the potential to enhance educational opportunities in India, and the proposed academic infrastructure. The committee will then provide recommendations within 45 days. Australia's Deakin University will be the first foreign tertiary education institution in the world to establish a campus in India. This is one of the two Universities (Deakin University and Wollongong University) which have high global rankings and have got clearance to establish a university campus in India.

Indian education, more with less

The Indian educational system has certainly its world-class achievements. The numbers of Indian students who gain admission in the top rung US educational institutions annually and the numbers of the Indian scientists and engineers employed in the US constitute a clear testimony to the Indian talent and Indian universities. In addition, the strong base of science and mathematics from the school level in India contrasts with the diffidence to engage in those studies in the US. However, these achievements are more in keeping with India's ability to "do more with less", rather than with a natural potential to "do even more with more". The gaps in the educational system can be seen at different levels from primary school education to higher university education.

The need for a massive transformation in the primary and secondary school educational systems together with strict enforcement of the right of every child for education is keenly felt in India. This is, however, a domain which is, and must remain as, the core competence of India. Foreign institutions would have little incentive or capability to play a role in this area. The fact that the pre-school and school years are also the years of solid foundational grounding in the Indian culture and Indian ethos, there is a case for the Indian institutions to display their moorings. Given this situation, this chapter focuses only on the higher education component of foreign institutional entry. The higher educational system has serious shortfalls in terms of infrastructure, faculty, and research direction.

Higher education, lower resources

The largest of the entities in the Indian educational system, the Indian Institutes of Technology (IITs) have an annual budget of around Rs 10,000 crore (USD 1.2 billion) from the Government of India. They have typical faculty strength of approximately 15,000 and student strength of around 100,000. In contrast, the US federal government has allocated approximately USD 271 billion for education, which includes funding for higher education as well as K-12 education in the year 2023. The faculty strength is of the order of 1.5 million and student strength of the order of 20 million. Research and development spending by academic institutions in the US totalled USD 191 billion in FY2023, an increase of 12.7 percent from FY2022. While clearly there are differences of scale and scope, these are particularly pronounced in funding channels and their scale as well as research budgets and their scope.

The Indian higher educational system has done particularly well to equip each of its students to higher education or higher research abroad. What the Indian system failed to do is to create a base of fundamental research and development in its institutions in India that could serve as the further developmental grounds for the Indian talent. Even today, the breakthrough research continues to get done in the university laboratories of US, Japan, and Europe. The Nobel prizes continue to get largely won by professors of US and European laboratories (despite several Indian researchers working in those laboratories). The entry of foreign educational institutions should address this fundamental infrastructure, research, and resource gap rather than aim at focusing only on run of the mill degree award and executive development programs. Figure 7.2 shows the achievements and challenges in Indian education.

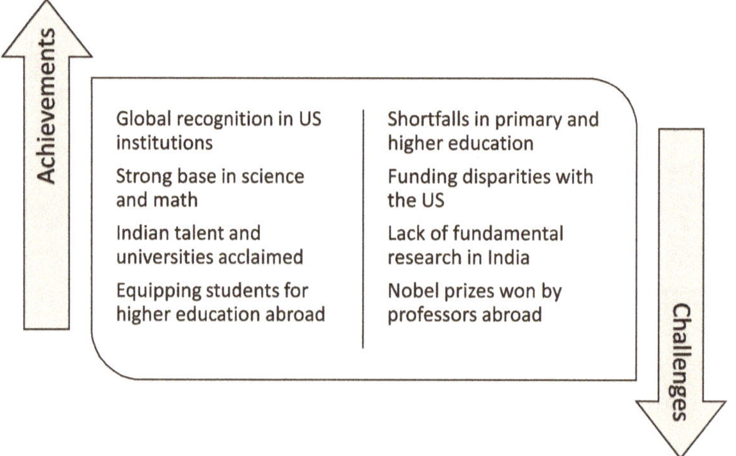

Figure 7.2: Achievements and Challenges in Indian Education

Building a new research ecosystem

Foreign educational institutions can make a significant contribution in building a new research ecosystem in the Indian educational institutions, provided their entry is directed well. The work in the foreign laboratories is continuously focused on the fundamentals of matter and biology, oftentimes exploring the linkages. For example, by the time India began looking at genetics, epigenetics has been taken up in a big way in US laboratories. Interdisciplinary research is an institutional approach to provide new solutions. Microrobotics for less invasive surgery, nano-structured meta-materials, development of new materials such as graphine, ultra-sensitive diagnostics, human protein sequencing, personality genetics, amino acid studies, solar energy development, and so on. While not all research makes it to commercialization and while some is hyperbole in advance, the fact remains that many new problem solving directions are emerging from the US, European or Japanese academic research.

The dilemma or disconnect for the Indian educational system lies in having a valuable stock of academically trained scientists and technologists in India who necessarily have to find a research base in the advanced laboratories of the US, Japan or Europe. Clearly, the value proposition for the foreign educational institutions must lie in accessing Indian talent without barriers and for the purpose creating the requisite laboratory infrastructure, research processes and information exchanges in India. This would certainly be a more complex process than sourcing products or processes from India because of the sensitive nature of intellectual property generation and patenting issues. By acting innovatively and responsibly with enhanced capabilities of scientific and technical communication, the Indian talent can accelerate the publication and intellectual property record of the foreign universities. Overall, a new ecosystem needs to be the sine qua non for allowing the foreign educational institutions into India.

What the governments can do

The governments, state and central, should treat setting up of state-of-the-art laboratories under the Indian-foreign educational system on par with attracting global commercial manufacturing and research proposals. Liberal provisioning of land and supportive infrastructure such as roads, power and telecommunications would go a long way in creating world class educational and research infrastructure in India. The Government of India and the Indian universities can also address the intellectual property constraint or barrier through a vibrant intellectual property office (IPO) system in India. Proposals of collaboration between the Indian and foreign universities must specify clear domains of research and goals of development. Commercial viability should also be an area of focus for the initiatives through sponsored research projects.

Chapter 8

From IIMs to IILs

Management to Leadership

The Indian Institutes of Management (IIMs) have been the most successful of the Indian efforts to clone and absorb, and even excel over, the Western educational thought. The IIMs are a group of public autonomous institutes dedicated to management education in India. The institute at Calcutta was established first, on November 13, 1961, and was named Indian Institute of Management Calcutta or IIM Calcutta. It was set up in collaboration with the MIT Sloan School of Management, the government of West Bengal, the Ford Foundation, and the Indian industry. The institute at Ahmedabad was established in the following month and was named Indian Institute of Management Ahmedabad. Like MIT Sloan in the case of IIM Calcutta, Harvard Business School played an important role in the initial stages of IIM Ahmedabad. The success of these two premier institutes prompted setting up of more Indian Institutes of Management (IIMs) from the 1970s. Today, India has twenty IIMs. In order of establishment, they are Calcutta (1961), Ahmedabad (1961), Bangalore (1973), Lucknow (1984), Kozhikode (1996), Indore (1996), Shillong (2007), Raipur (2010), Ranchi (2010), Rohtak (2010), Kashipur (2011), Tiruchirappalli (2011), Udaipur (2011), Amritsar (2015), Bodh Gaya (2015), Nagpur (2015), Sambalpur (2015), Sirmaur (2015), Vishakhapatnam (2015) and Jammu (2016). NITIE, established in 1963 in Mumbai for training in industrial engineering was converted into an IIM in 2023, making it the twenty-first IIM. The success of the IIMs triggered the mushrooming of standalone management schools and establishment of management divisions within general and technical educational institutions.

The IIMs offer a wide variety of management courses. They were established with the objectives of providing high quality management education and to assist industry through research and consulting services. By and large, the IIMs have fulfilled the vision and objectives. IIMs are among the most prestigious and elite business schools in India. Like the Indian Institutes of Technology (IITs) which attract the best school leaving talent through nation-wide Joint Entrance Examination (JEE), the IIMs attract the best graduate talent through their Common Admission Test (CAT). The IIMs primarily offer postgraduate, doctoral, and executive education programs. The two-year Postgraduate Program in Management (PGP), offering the Postgraduate Diploma in Management (PGDM), is the flagship program across all IIMs. Some IIMs also offer a one-year Postgraduate Program for experienced executives. Some IIMs offer the Fellow Program in Management (FPM), a doctoral program. The Postgraduate Diploma and Fellowship are equivalent to MBA and Ph.D., respectively. Many IIMs also offer short-term executive education courses and part-time programs. Figure 8.1 illustrates the key features of IIMs.

Figure 8.1: Key Features of Indian Institutes of Management (IIMs)

Expectations and realities

According to IIM Ahmedabad (IIMA), students admitted to the Post-graduate Program in the past have had scholastic achievements in different disciplines such as arts, commerce, science, and professional streams such as medicine, engineering, and agriculture. Some of the qualities which characterize past students include high levels of initiative and energy, capacity for hard work, strong task orientation, willingness to learn, and a temperament suitable for teamwork. The PGP classes have had a mix of fresh graduates and persons with work experience. Among the recent PGP students, a significant proportion has had full-time paid work experience of more than six months after their graduation. The influx of experienced graduates into the IIM stream reflects the gap between the expectations developed in fresh students by the IIM education and the experienced maturity levels that most brick-and-mortar organizations need. The IIMs typically prepare the students to leapfrog over the first executive steps to become managers straightaway. The fundamentals of products, processes and the marketplace are therefore not mastered to the requisite extent by the management graduates. Many times, the intelligence and grasp of the management graduates enables them to overcome the lack of frontline experience. Even so, the gaps between the demands posed by the role intricacy and peer group imbalance in organizations on the one hand, and the aspirations fuelled by the strategy oriented management education and the initial jumpstart of the career, on the other hand remain high.

Despite this realization and the influx of experienced personnel into IIM studentship, even if the majority is with experience of a few years, the challenges of expectation-reality gap and aspiration-delivery gap have not dimmed. The practical circumstances force that, out of the thousands of IIM alumni that join the ranks of industry and business each year, only a few become the most successful entrepreneurs or most effective leaders, managing total enterprises, and meeting all the benchmarks of popularly recognized success and effectiveness. In a career, spanning four decades leading to enterprise leadership, so much emphasis is put on just two years of management education at the base of the career, which is subject further to the rollercoaster of organizational dynamics. One way of looking at the elite management education system of India is that the IIMs teach leadership to the unprepared far too early. IIM qualifications catapult their students into managerial positions straightaway. This denies them the benefit of the experience of moving through laboratory, manufacturing, or field work, and in the process makes them lag in authentic leadership potential. Given that India's quest for global economic position requires leadership in multiple domains, clearly time is opportune to define the limits to management education and explore the next frontier of leadership education.

Early genesis and emerging logic

Despite the adverse image India's post-independence socialistic polity has, many of the more progressive institutional initiatives of India owe their origin and inspiration to administrative analysis and political wisdom. The Indian Institutes of Technology (IITs) were established by the Government of India, under the leadership of Jawaharlal Nehru, the first Prime Minister of India who believed in scientific and technological self-reliance. The IITs were set up as a group of autonomous engineering and technology-oriented institutes of higher education, declared as "institutions of national importance". They were created progressively from 1951 to develop a talent base of scientists and engineers, to support the economic and social development of India. Today, India boasts of twenty-three IITs. The establishment of the IIMs was also envisioned and initiated by the Indian Government, based on the recommendation of the Planning Commission. India grew rapidly in the 1950s, and in the late 1950s the Commission started facing difficulties in finding suitable managers for the large number of public sector enterprises that were being established in India as a part of its industrial policy. To solve this problem, the Planning Commission in 1959 invited Professor George Robbins of the University of California to help in setting up an All India Institute of Management Studies. Based on his recommendations, the Indian government decided to set up two elite management institutes, Indian Institutes of Management, Calcutta, and Ahmedabad.

India today has a civil service cadre of over 50,000, manning the huge all-India governmental and administrative apparatus. These belong primarily to the all-India services and the central services. The all-India services consist of the Indian Administrative Service (IAS), Indian Police Service (IPS) and Indian Forest Service (IFoS). The personnel of these services are allotted state cadres and primarily work with the State Governments. They also serve on deputation to the Central Government. The Indian Administrative Service, with its federal nature, forms the backbone of the delivery of basic services and poverty alleviation programs. The seven central services comprise Indian Audit & Accounts Service (IA&AS), Indian Foreign Service (IFS), Indian Revenue Service (Income Tax), Indian Revenue Service (Customs & Central Excise), Indian Railway Personnel Service (IRPS), Indian Railway Traffic Service (IRTS) and Indian Postal Service (IPoS). The cadre of all these ten services is perhaps insufficient to cater to the needs of the huge 1.4 billion population and their development needs in India.

India has 58 Union ministries and 93 departments and over 766 administrative districts, each of which requires several individual service heads. In 1951, there were five PSUs under the ownership of the central government sector in India. By March 2023, the number of such government entities had increased to 389. India also has over 100,000 joint stock, public limited and private limited companies, each of which requires multiple corporate officers and enterprise leaders. The leadership pool is supplied by scientists, engineers, professionals, some of them with formal management qualifications; all of them acquired at the starting phase of their careers. Most of the leadership capabilities and competencies are acquired by these officers as they progress through their three-to-four-decade careers. The environmental context, in terms of political, social, demographic, economic, business, and technological trends, changes significantly every five years or so. It is a moot point if the currently available educational structures, including the management capstone education offered and acquired typically in, and by, one's mid-twenties would be adequate in one's latter half of the career, i.e., between forty-five and sixty-five years of age, when the leadership impact is expected to be the maximum. There is, typically, a mid-career inflexion point in one's leadership journey which is completely unattended to in the current educational system.

Breaking the journey

The mid-career point, say the period between forty and forty-five years of age (corresponding to fifteen to twenty years of experience) is the inflexion point when typically, a mature manager begins to morph into a potential leader. By then, a successful manager would have reached a level of functional mastery and cross-functional capability demonstrated by successful headship of a function, division, or a region. What lies ahead is the opportunity to head a business with profit and loss responsibility and later the total corporation. In some cases, the emerging leader would be required to even start up an entirely new business or open a new region for the corporation. The leadership skills for this transformational journey would be significantly different in terms of developing a business or enterprise vision, formulating a transformation strategy, and executing it through a leadership that walks the vision and strategy. The mature manager's skills of orderly resource management, compliance to established systems and procedures and programmed people management would be necessary but would fall short of the leadership needs. Non-recognition of this inflexion requirement causes managers to continue to act as managers even when they are catapulted to leadership positions.

The answer to this lies in the managers and the companies as well as the civil servants and the governments retooling the mature managerial talent base and transforming it into an emerging leadership talent pool at the above identified mid-career point. The transformation requires the reinforcement of the managerial skills in the new-generation and next-generation contexts and the absorption of what it takes to be a leader in the changing environmental context. For example, the contemporary marketing head must understand the importance of social networking and how it could further change in future and the transformative products and services that are needed to leverage the social networking. Amazon leadership, for example, transformed the industry through electronic book, Kindle and online digital book libraries, leveraging the Internet and telecommunication technologies for its universal marketplace, and built for itself an industry dominating position. Online music technologies and cloud platforms demonstrate the need for leadership to transform lives through transformed corporations. This transformation requires the mature managers to shed the past partially and take on leadership development fully. Figure 8.2 illustrates the skills required for transformation from manager to leader.

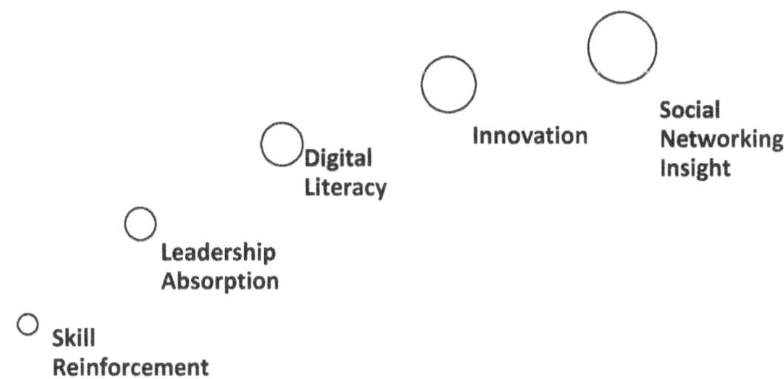

Figure 8.2: Skills Required for Transformation from Manager to Leader

Indian Institutes of Leadership (IILs)

Just as the IITs and IIMs provided a fundamental and lasting breakthrough for India in the scientific, engineering and management education from the 1950s and 1960s, a new network of Indian Institutes of Leadership (IILs) would mark a pioneering transformation in the buildup of leadership development in India. The IILs, like the IITs and IIMs, should be deemed institutes of national importance, and set up as autonomous institutions under the Act of Indian Parliament. The admission to the IILs should be open only to the practising civil servants or corporate managers in the age group of forty to forty-five years, with a corresponding experience of fifteen to twenty years. The admission should be open to mature managers who qualify through a Common Admission Test Customized for Leadership. The admission should also be open to those managers who are sponsored as well as those who resigned from their managerial services, with appropriate years of experience as stipulated. The Government, the industry and the industry associations have a role in supporting the establishment and ramp-up of IILs. It also requires that IIMs confine themselves only to their current educational formats and not open new leadership course streams for highly experienced candidates. However, IITs and IIMs should be encouraged to establish either on their own or in partnership with the government and the industry discrete IILs.

The curriculum of IILs should obviously be innovative and challenging and state-of-the-art in terms of adaptation to the dynamic external environment. It should focus on transforming functional managers into business leaders without losing the core technical and professional strengths. Capabilities and competencies to start and grow startups, undertake green field expansions and diversifications, achieve globalization, and leverage pioneering technologies should be the unique deliverables of the programs. The curriculum should promote networking between industrial leaders and civil servants as well as between entrepreneurial leaders and professional leaders. The sponsoring corporations should treat the study period of twelve to eighteen months as paid sabbatical period and seek no direct relationship between the study stream and the company domain; on the other hand, the companies should see the IIL programs as multifaceted leadership development initiatives. The faculty competencies should also be commensurate with the lofty and challenging goals of the IILs; the best of business leaders from India and abroad should constitute the core faculty with fulltime involvement. The IILs would be as transformative in India's leadership drive as the IITs and IIMs had so far been and would continue to be in India's educational drive.

Chapter 9

An Ecosystem for Fundamental Research

An Essential Paradigm for India

Nobel Prizes for sciences (Physiology or Medicine, Physics and Chemistry) are some of the most coveted recognitions of fundamental research and discovery, globally. The Nobel Prize in Physiology or Medicine 2023 was awarded to Katalin Karikó and Drew Weissman for their discoveries concerning nucleoside base modifications that enabled the development of effective mRNA vaccines against COVID-19. The Nobel Prize in Physics 2023 was awarded jointly to Pierre Agostini, Ferenc Krausz, and Anne L'Huillier for experimental methods that generate attosecond pulses of light for the study of electron dynamics in matter. The Nobel Prize in Chemistry 2023 was awarded jointly to Moungi G. Bawendi, Louis E. Brus, Aleksey Yekimov for the discovery and synthesis of quantum dots.

Katalin Karikó was affiliated, at the time of the award to Szeged University, Szeged, Hungary; and Drew Weissman to Penn Institute for RNA Innovations, University of Pennsylvania, Philadelphia, PA, USA. Pierre Agostini was affiliated, at the time of the award to The Ohio State University, Columbus, OH, USA, Ferenc Krausz to Max Planck Institute of Quantum Optics, Garching, Germany; Ludwig-Maximilians-Universität München, Munich, Germany and Anne L'Huillier to Lund University, Lund, Sweden. Moungi G. Bawendi was affiliated to Massachusetts Institute of Technology (MIT), Cambridge, MA, USA, Louis E. Brus to Columbia University, New York, NY, USA and Aleksey Yekimov to Nanocrystals Technology Inc., New York, NY, USA.

As almost always, the Nobel Prizes have been bagged by scientists working in the universities of advanced countries such as USA and European Union. An Indian scientist has not figured the prestigious Nobel roll call this year as well.

Indian Nobel Laureates

Sir CV Raman (1930) and Abdus Salam (1979) and Subramanyam Chandrasekhar (1983) in Physics, Ronald Ross (1902) and H Gobind Khorana (1968) in Physiology or Medicine, and Venkatraman Ramakrishnan (2009) in Chemistry are some of the prominent scientific luminaries from India who won Nobel Prizes in Sciences (excluding literature and economic sciences). Given that in terms of numbers India has probably the largest number of colleges, institutions and universities offering scientific and technical education, the very small number of Indians amongst Nobel Laureates and the non-appearance of Indian institutions in terms of affiliations at the time of award is quite disappointing. It is even more disappointing that although thousands of bright Indian scholars leave each year for higher order scientific education, including doctoral and post-doctoral studies in the USA and EU, the number of such Indians who became Nobel Laureates is even smaller.

This situation is to be read with the fact that in 2023, in the ranking of the Top 500 universities by ARWU (Academic Ranking of World Universities), only one Indian educational institution, the Indian Institute of Science figures, with a ranking between 300 and 400. Harvard University tops the ranking list for the 21st year, followed by Stanford and MIT. Out of the top 30 ranked universities, the United States had 20 different universities on the list. Mainland China now has 35 universities entering top 1000 for the first time. ARWU, also known as Shanghai Rankings, considers every university that has any Nobel Laureates, field medalists, highly cited researchers, or papers published in Nature or Science. In addition, universities with significant number of papers indexed by the Science Citation Index-

Expanded (SCIE) and the Social Science Citation Index (SSCI) are also included. In total, more than 1,000 universities are ranked, and the best 500 are published on the web. Universities are also ranked by several indicators of academic or research performance, and the per capita academic performance of an institution. For each indicator, the highest scoring institution is assigned a score of 100, and other institutions are calculated as a percentage of the top score.

Indian University Scenario

India has around 1,113 universities, including 21 Indian Institutes of Management (IIMs), 23 Indian Institutes of Technology (IITs) and 31 National Institutes of Technology (NITs). Each university, except the IIMs, IITs and NITs as well as some specialized universities tends to have several colleges attached to it; an average reported figure is 300 colleges per university. All the universities and colleges except the few dedicated to management education teach and conduct research in science and engineering. The Council of Scientific and Industrial Research (CSIR) is the largest Government funded, autonomous R&D Organization in India, having 37 laboratories which cover, among others, biological sciences, physical sciences, chemical sciences, and engineering sciences. As of March 31, 2022, CSIR's research and development capabilities are represented by a workforce of approximately 3,521 active scientists, complemented by around 4,162 technical and support staff.

As per the most recent OECD report, India has secured the fourth position in the ranking of countries by doctoral graduates' production, generating just over 24,000 doctorate holders. The United States leads this list with 68,000 graduates, claiming the top spot. This is quantitatively impressive considering that all the OECD countries are reportedly producing 100,000 PhDs each year. Numbers possibly tell only less than half of the story, at least as far as India is concerned. While the doctoral programs in the USA are focused on the cutting edge of science and engineering, with a fair degree of association with Nobel Laureates and laboratories undertaking fundamental research, the Indian PhDs are handicapped by the lack of such leading-edge associations. In addition, lack of laboratories committed to fundamental research in India for post-doctoral and research employment in public sector or private sector further constrains even those who have passion for research in India. The OECD report also revealed that less than 2 percent of the world's population has a doctorate degree today. Figure 9.1 shows the Indian university scenario.

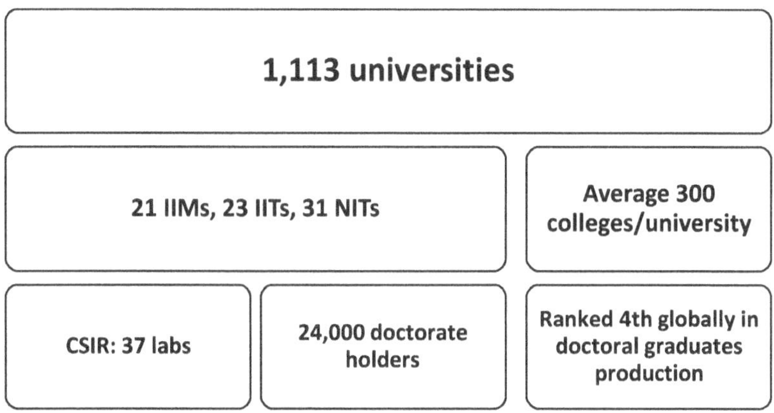

Figure 9.1: Indian University Scenario

IIFRs for a Research Ecosystem

India has less than 1 percent of its graduates enrolling for Ph D programs. The brightest of graduates, in fact, migrate to the advanced universities in the US and Europe for PhD programs. There is a clear need to address the fundamental research paradigm in India not merely to retain more PhD talent but more fundamentally to raise the state of discovery and innovation in India. With India harmonizing its intellectual property regime with the world order, the previously held concerns on protecting discoveries and inventions out of India have considerably reduced. There must, therefore, be concerted efforts in, and for,

India to participate in cutting edge research. Rather than spread itself thin, India could implement a phased plan to establish the foundations of fundamental research, starting with physical and chemical sciences, followed by engineering sciences and biological sciences.

The research ecosystem can take roots and grow only when the industry integrates the fundamental research in its operations and is proactive in contributing to the establishment of centres of fundamental research in India. Like the industry and business are expected to contribute financially to fulfill corporate social responsibility (CSR), there would need to be contributions to fulfill corporate innovation responsibility (CIR). A part of the research ecosystem should include a major initiative by the Government of India to set up a chain of Indian Institutes of Fundamental Research (IIFRs), on the lines of the IITs and IIMs, but exclusively focused on postgraduate education and doctoral and post-doctoral research. In addition, two developments in the Indian educational system that are potentially on their way must be restructured and leveraged for the benefit of fundamental research.

The first is the entry of corporate houses into Indian research-oriented education. Instead of focusing on run-of-the-mill programs, business houses should partner with the IIFRs to establish research schools of excellence and/or provide grants and chairs to encourage fundamental researchers. If they wish to set up their own institutes, they must be their own institutes of fundamental research. Secondly, foreign universities that want to enter India must be asked to set up at least one centre of fundamental research in each of their Indian centres as part of their physical campus programs in India. Just as India has delivered substantial value in global outsourcing of information technology and manufacturing, India would deliver significant value for foreign universities networking into India for fundamental research. A combination of Government sponsored IIFRs, public sector and private sector corporate sponsored research centers and foreign universities' extension research schools should provide the winning formula for a pervasive ecosystem for fundamental research in India. Figure 9.2 shows the ways to enhance fundamental research in India.

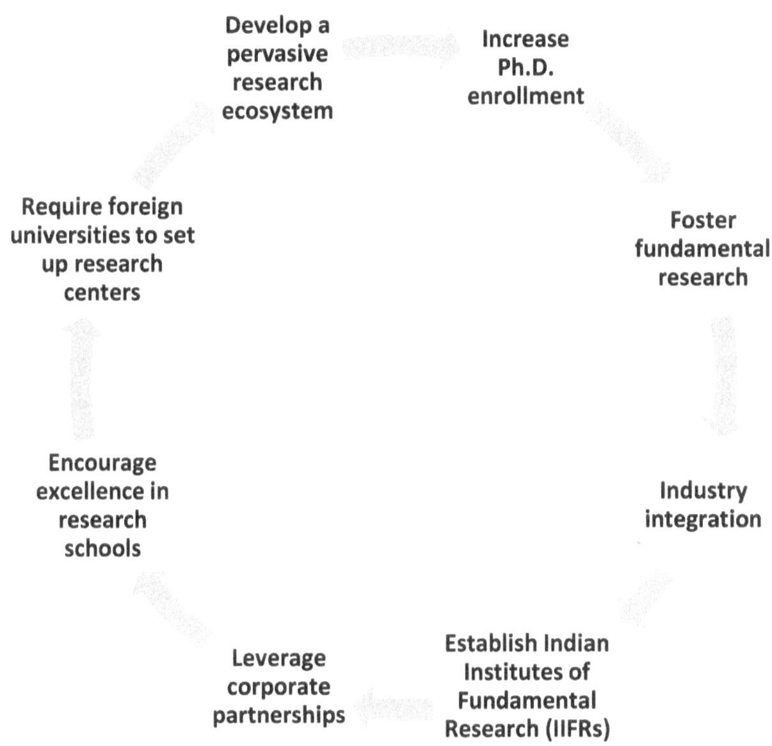

Figure 9.2: Enhancing Fundamental Research in India

Research is a Passion

Basic to fundamental research is the fact that research is a passion, and not an employment or a business input. True researchers tend to be passionate in the field of discovery and invention. Neither age and gender nor nationality and geography have any relevance to the unending quest for new discoveries and inventions. Amongst the hundreds of Nobel Laureates, 17 years is the age of the youngest Laureate and 97 is the age of the oldest;

59 years is the average. In fact, over 50 Laureates are younger than 40 years, with most of them being in Physics. As Dr Higgs's continuing work demonstrates, fundamental research is a lifetime passion. Similarly, it is truly multinational; if a world-class research ecosystem exists in any nation, world-class researchers would migrate to that nation, as a large nation like US and a small nation like Sweden equally exemplify.

Research takes extraordinarily extended time and intense effort that cannot be ordinarily rewarded. It is even more so with fundamental research. It drills down to unexplored hidden depths of knowledge but also connects seemingly unconnected domains of knowledge. The 2013 Nobel Prizes in Chemistry and Physiology demonstrate the importance of cross-functional knowledge, especially computer modeling or transportation modeling, in understanding complex chemical and biological activities. The God Particle (Higgs boson) research could not have happened but for the massive investment and effort involved in establishing the Large Hadron Collider at CERN in Switzerland. While India does need to go a long way in fulfilling certain basic economic, industrial, and social growth needs through considerable investments, India cannot also afford to ignore the need and responsibility to invest in establishing and nurturing an ecosystem for fundamental research. Fundamental research will lead to a truly fundamental transformation towards a leadership role in global scientific and engineering domains for India.

Chapter 10

Management & Leadership

At the Cost of Science & Technology?

From being a staid domain a few decades ago to becoming a glamorous domain, management & leadership (M&L) have emerged as gateways to career progress and organizational ascendancy, even to scientists and technologists. Despite any number of achievements in science & technology (S&T), such as the successful launch of indigenous cryogenic space rocket, Mangalyaan Mission, Chandrayaan Mission, and Aditya Solar Mission by the Indian Space Research Organization (ISRO) and the national pride and international recognition such scientific and technological achievements bring to India, there is no let-up in the preference for management and leadership courses, both in pre-career and in in-career stages. While the educational and course preferences tend to be a matter of supply and demand as well as job potential, an emerging economy such as India cannot afford to leave the knowledge dynamics entirely to market fancies. A nation will have a true meritocracy when domains are geared to continuously develop new knowledge, and to continuously expand the body of the overall knowledge base, in the process integrating the new knowledge and making the existing knowledge contemporaneously relevant.

The craze of sorts for M&L, which essentially meant students and professionals moving away from further specialization in S&T courses (at postgraduate or research levels) to M&L courses (at postgraduate or fellow levels), has made advanced countries lose their some of the competitive edge. It has prompted some of such countries to welcome overseas students and professionals from S&T streams into their nations. Emerging countries such as India and China benefitted from the importance given to S&T in their curricula. Amongst all the Asian countries, including China, Japan, and Korea, only India has favoured the growth of M&L streams to a great extent, essentially as an offshoot of adopting the Western education model. While this need not be disparaged, movement of top-flight talent from S&T to M&L needs to be discouraged. S&T, rightly so, have higher entry barriers for learning and mastery, compared to M&L. Lower entry barriers to learning coupled with higher job opportunities could lead to distortions in India's talent pool and industrial endeavours, particularly at a time India requires the ultimate push to become an economic superpower. To restore S&T to pride of place, the important facets of being an S&T professional need to be understood by students and educational institutions as well as recognized and rewarded by industrial organizations.

Touchstone of solidity

Any knowledge domain that raises expectations must eventually live up to the expectations of contributions to society in terms of the domain knowledge and its technological applicability. S&T undoubtedly qualifies as a critical knowledge domain under this criterion. The body of knowledge under S&T continually grows, oftentimes in exponential spurts, transforming society and quality of life. The S&T knowledge is an eclectic combination of principles, laws, logic, and mathematics, leading to quantification of physical, chemical, and biological models. There is a relevant and sustainable correlation between publications, patents, theory, and practice in S&T, making them truly holistic knowledge domains. Science creates theory out of experiments and uses experiments to validate theory. Technology applies science to design, manufacture and deliver products or services. In contrast, the body of knowledge under M&L seems to increase at best once in a decade, and the total body of knowledge of the last several decades of organized M&L can be summarized under a handful of concepts. The M&L knowledge is predominantly based on behaviours and couched in linguistic expressions. The real expansion of knowledge in M&L, which is very low relative to S&T, is magnified by rather creative expressions and sporadic case analyses; very little is based on statistically representative research. Management creates repetitive theories on age-old principles like planning, organizing, staffing, directing, coordination, controlling and budgeting. Leadership looks at personalities to weave modelling theories around stylistic syndromes.

S&T requires M&L for optimized commercialization but not necessarily always. Without S&T, however, M&L is completely superfluous; in fact, M&L is purposeless without S&T. Whether companies that wade through financial management or countries that are resurrected after economic collapse, they are dependent on science and technology. If New Delhi's T3 airport of yesterday or Bengaluru's T2 airport of today received rave reviews, despite managerial delays, the technological concept and execution grandeur are responsible in no small measure. It is somewhat of a misrepresentation that S&T and M&L are distinct, and it is an even more of misrepresentation that S&T requires M&L to optimize itself. S&T approach which is based on review of current knowledge, logic of new hypothesis and validation through experiments has the basic managerial principles integral to the approach. S&T, once established, accepts no ambiguity. The basic principles of S&T whether it is the Periodic Table of Elements, the Boyle's Law, or the Iron-Carbon Diagram, do not change over time. S&T is absolute in a universal sense. A deep sense of review and a tremendous level of experimentation make the principles rock-solid. In contrast, all M&L principles are contextually flexible and iteratively reversible and merely firm-specific or person-influenced (for example, integration is good for some, integration is bad for some; conglomeration has been good in the 1950s, bad in the 1980s, again great in 2010s, and so on). Figure 10.1 shows the comparison between S&T and M&L.

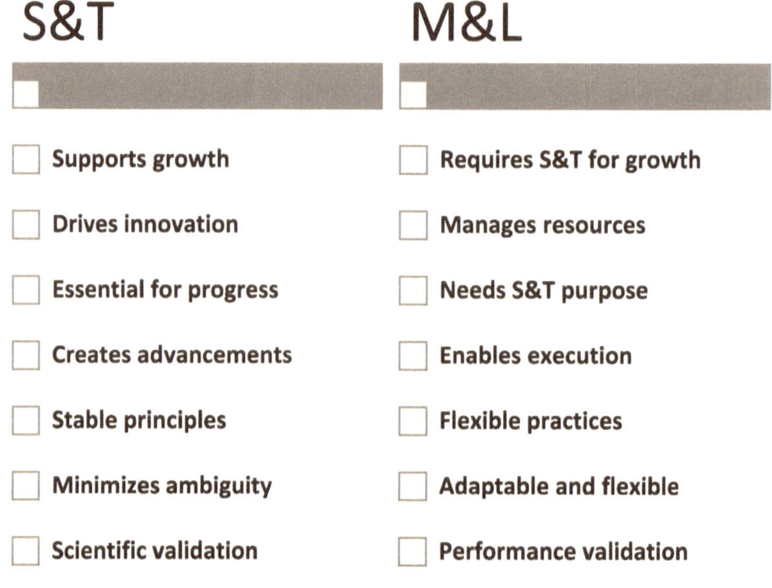

Figure 10.1: Comparison Between S&T and M&L

Linear versus circular

Science and technology have a linear (and exponential) development track. Each S&T development builds on the past for a new future, rather than revert to the past. Management and leadership, in contrast, are steeped in rediscovery. From time to time, old M&L concepts are simply refurbished and repositioned, from time to time. The flight of talent to such refurbishment and repositioning of management and leadership instead of staying with science and technology is a matter of concern. Having attracted such S&T talent, the inability of the M&L domains to become linear and exponential in genuine knowledge accretion is a matter of greater concern. The question that dispassionate analysts face is whether M&L streams contribute materially relevant value or just add some transient flamboyance to basic S&T. The first two decades of independent India had no institutes of management or even business management courses, yet the country saw significant industrialization. The best of India's talent went into the graduate engineer schemes of technological giants. The strength of these industrial undertakings today is based on these talented scientific and engineering corps which grew the companies and grew with the companies. Officers of the Indian Administrative Services were some of the best managers and leaders then. One would, therefore, like to see better value addition from the proliferation of M&L streams.

This phenomenon of early-stage fundamental development on the base of science and technology is common to technology leaders of America, Inc as also to several Asian countries, such as Japan, Korea, and China. From the early Toyota Production System that originated on the automobile shopfloor to the Minimalist Design Philosophy that emerged from classy electronic devices, it is science and technology of design, manufacture and delivery that has been presumptively positioned as management and leadership models. From time to time, newer phraseology such as lean, six-sigma is used to reposition the philosophy of 'minimal input-maximal value' that is inherent at each level of S&T through the ages. Even the interpersonal facets of M&L are just simple principles of balanced living that are ingrained in the spiritual and philosophical treatises of various religions from times immemorial. The relative paucity of new M&L thoughts is due to the limited nature of enquiry, which is confined to the four types of human-machine interfaces; human-machine, machine-machine, human-machine and human-human. S&T, on the other hand, is in an endless pursuit of seemingly inexplicable and indeterminate natural phenomena, in terms of physical, chemical, and biological models of the universe. The greater the talent concentration on S&T, as opposed to M&L, the greater could be the value generation and wealth creation in a nation through the unravelling of the natural mysteries and discovery, and subsequent perfection of solutions for them.

Rediscovering M&L

To be fundamentally value-accretive and practically effective, M&L must be considered as subservient adjuncts to S&T domains rather than as substitute or revisionist superior domains. The key M&L learning factors need to be integrated into S&T curricula. As part of several decades of practical experience, I had the occasion to interact with hundreds of management graduates, managers and leaders employed in industry or services sectors; not one has admitted having implemented the courses taught in the two-year management programs, be it, for example, advanced statistics, operations research, portfolio theory, signalling theory, reliability models, and the like. Given that the engineering degree program in India is of four years durations, it makes little sense to unlearn the core S&T and spend another two years in learning fancied M&L, most of which it is never applied in any case. Given that good management and leadership is an integral part of science and technology, it would make better sense to integrate certain core management and leadership subjects, not exceeding eight in number (one in each of the eight semesters), as part of S&T domain learning. These could be statistics, economics, accounting, and finance as the four core subjects, and operations, marketing, strategy, and responsibility as the four application subjects.

Those who are committed to M&L as their life's passion must be prepared to go through the full five-year professional certification programs in management and leadership, as economists, mathematicians and accountants go through. Only then, the exponents of management and leadership, whether in academics or industry, will be challenged to develop and grow as a self-sustaining discipline rather than as a discipline that piggybacks on other disciplines, and unwittingly makes the core disciplines ignored. M&L as a stand-alone discipline will have its own research and self-development paradigms, to be relevant to the nation as a separate knowledge continuum. This, coupled with the earlier proposed strategy of graduate and postgraduate S&T programs being self-sufficient with their basic M&L knowledge, would ensure that the investments made in S&T are preserved and flight of talent from S&T is avoided. Many institutes and universities making hay on capstan management programs will be disappointed with this approach but India, as an emerging nation, will immensely benefit from S&T investments, in both education and industry, fulfilling their potential. Probably, the famed IIMs can take the lead by stopping piggybacking on the IITs for the core talent with their two-year MBA programs and start standing alone in the fields of management and leadership through new five-year integrated MBA programs. Figure 10.2 summarizes the way to rediscover M&L.

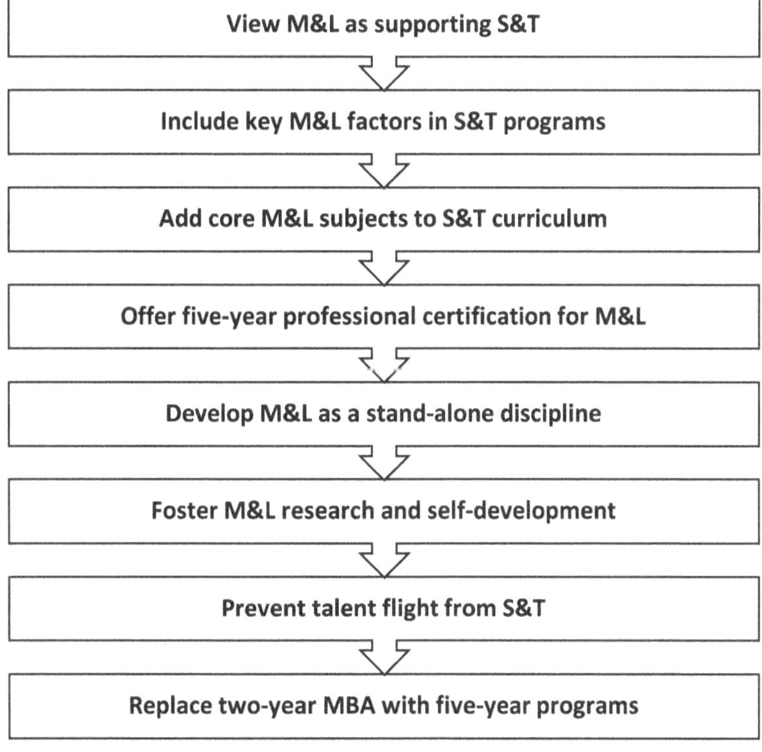

Figure 10.2: Ways to Rediscover M&L

Chapter 11

Scientific Temper and Technological Perfection

The Driver of National Competitive Advantage

Organizations contribute to a nation's wealth and national competitive advantage. India has recognized the importance of science and technology and created the department of science and technology. It is, however, a moot point if the fervour of science and technology truly pervades India, Inc; for, if it were, India would have been far less import dependent on products of high technology and far more export competitive in terms of India-made high technology products. Part of the reason is due to early digression of talent, focus and investments from the demanding aspects of science and technology to the glimmering aspects of management and administration. This chapter postulates that establishment of scientific temper and technological perfection should be pursued as national core competencies to derive national competitive advantage.

Complex qualities

With decades of unrelenting publication of management thought, it is expected in management folklore that members of an organization must possess all humanly possible qualities, referred to often as competencies, capabilities, skills, abilities, traits, and attitudes. These are often classified into hard skills and soft skills, as well as into operating skills and strategic skills. The prescribed human qualities are several, to quote a few professional knowledge, conceptual skills, analytical skills, and interpersonal skills. As higher levels of organization are considered, other additional qualities are prescribed which include, for example, foresight, vision, integrity, ethics, intuition, and charisma. My study, in fact, listed over 100 human qualities that a leader, and potential leaders, must possess. As a result of this trend (or fad), programs to develop these myriad qualities have burgeoned into a management learning and development industry by itself!

A parallel phenomenon relates to professional specialization or functional specialization. This has, in fact, become the very organizational core of socio-economic and business-industrial infrastructure. The number of professions is no longer limited to a few; it has vastly expanded beyond the traditional research, procurement, manufacturing, quality, and selling domains to spawn additional domains, for example operations, logistics, legal, secretarial, marketing, information technology. In addition, professionalization has got merged with product lines to include automobile engineers, oncologists, pharmacists, chemists, and the like. The matrix of growing professions and product lines has led to an exponential proliferation of qualities which each of these specialist and generic professions must possess. Rather than myriad qualities, two pristine qualities – scientific temper and technological perfection – are all that are required for national competitive advantage.

Simple differentiators

For sustainable success and perpetual growth, organizations need to have high quality human resources. At one level, the more scientists, and engineers an organization has the more likely would be its competitive advantage. This does not mean that organizations should have only scientists and engineers (or technologists) or that other professionals such as managers and accountants are not important. In fact, even more important than the numbers, is the organization-wide presence of certain mesmeric and differentiated qualities that science and technology stand for. These are scientific passion and technological perfection. These help organizations discover, design, and deliver not merely products and services but new ways of doing any of the organizational or business processes. As much as the calibre and number of scientists, engineers and technologists in any organization, the extent of scientific fervour and technological perfection across the organization is the key differentiator.

Science and technology (or, engineering) are closely related and often have interdependent and overlapping functions. Science enables fundamental discoveries while engineering designs the equipment and products and makes manufacturing and delivery possible. Science requires sophisticated engineering and technological infrastructure to deliver. Higgs boson particle (God Particle) could be discovered only because of equipment made with unprecedented engineering and technological sophistication such as the Large Hadron Collider of 27-kilometer length. Stem cell discoveries would not be of any avail without cryogenics and cryogenic equipment. By the same taken, without discoveries in materials science nanotechnology developments would not be feasible. Science and technology are so closely interrelated that it would be unnecessary to delineate the respective functions. What can be delineated, however, are the basic qualities of the two disciplines.

Scientific temper

Pandit Jawaharlal Nehru, the first Prime Minister of independent India was the first to articulate the concept of scientific temper. In his landmark book "The Discovery of India" he advocated reliance on observed facts and not on pre-conceived notions, the search for truth and new knowledge, and a refusal to accept anything without testing and trial as some of the important characteristics of scientific temper. He proposed that scientific temper was required not merely for the application of science but for life itself and the solution of many of its problems. The concept of scientific temper is critically required for organizations which most of the times get caught up in whirlpools of pre-conceived notions, convenient propositions, and ad-hoc reactions. Scientific temper needs to be an individual and organizational way of thinking and acting that uses a scientific method, of observing physical reality and drawing conclusions or hypothesizing the abstract possibilities and validating potential outcomes.

Scientific temper is an attitude to life that integrates logic, discussion, debate, and analysis to arrive at the best possible conclusions. Inherent to scientific temper is the ability to think and communicate. Organizations, schools and colleges or businesses and governments, should promote positive thoughtfulness and constructive expressiveness to institutionalize scientific temper. The economic benefits of scientific temper are many; Nehru's scientific temper led to setting up of the Indian Institutes of Technology and national research laboratories, establishment of several heavy industries and construction of multiple dams within a few years of Indian independence. Leaders with scientific temper would similarly institutionalize science and technology in their organizations. More than that, they will facilitate processes of scientific enquiry all through the organization leading to logical decision making, structured execution and objective monitoring of results. Figure 11.1 summarises the key attributes of scientific temper.

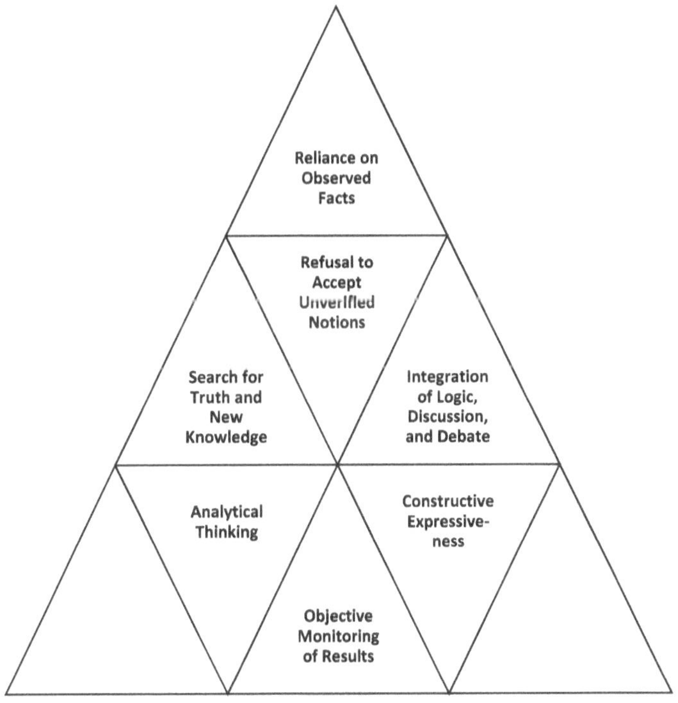

Figure 11.1: Key Attributes of Scientific Temper

Technological perfection

Compared to scientific temper, technological perfection is a moving concept; moving, of course, to higher levels of perfection every period. Perfection is defined as having everything that is necessary, and without faults or weaknesses; in one sense, the highest level of quality attainable at any point of time. The limits of perfection are set by the limits of technology available at any point of time and given that scientific temper causes humans to push technology ever to newer limits, the limits of perfection also set to move continuously upwards. Whether it is the power to weight ratios and fuel efficiency and emission levels of automobiles or is the imaging capabilities of scanners and surgical precision of radio-knifes and lasix lasers, technological perfection continuously pushes up the accomplishments of devices and equipment as well as man-machine systems.

Like scientific temper, technological perfection is an attitude to life that integrates aesthetics with performance, durability with reliability, and economy with efficiency. Technology tends more often to be continuously incremental and periodically breakthrough. Cost and affordability constitute the twin ballasts that stabilize technological randomness. Scientific temper that triggers technological quest also governs the irrelevant technological perfection. The economic benefits of technological perfection are many. Without achieving better fits and tolerances as well as better finishes and efficiencies, Japanese automobiles would not have been world leaders. Higher levels of technology bring higher levels of service but also higher levels of profligate consumerism and adverse consumption. Scientific temper enables individuals and organizations to draw an appropriate balance between cost and consumption. Figure 11.2 illustrates the key attributes of technological perfection.

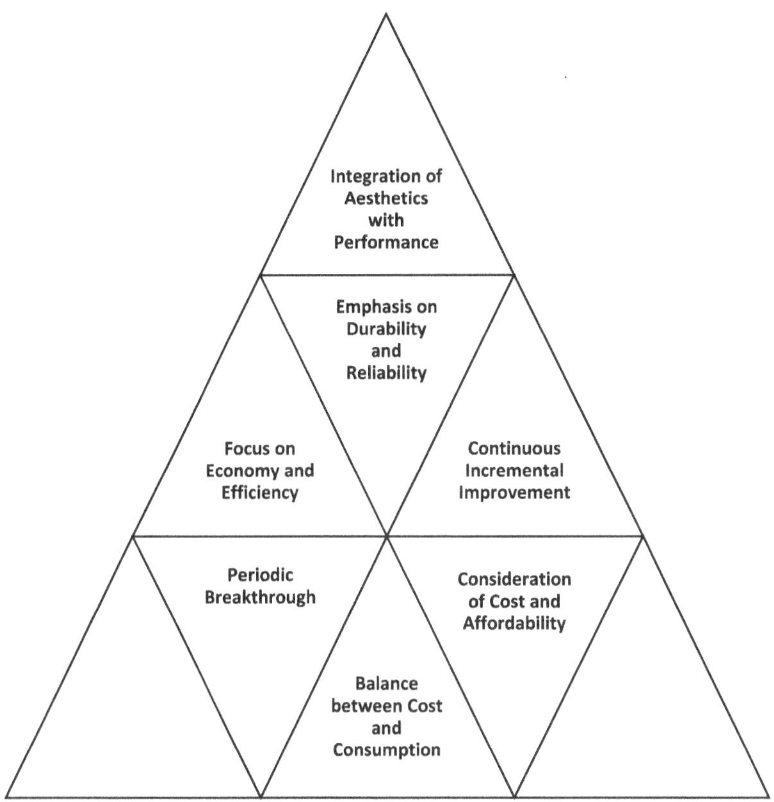

Figure 11.2: Key Attributes of Technological Perfection

Humanism

There is a school of thought that clinical application of scientific temper and unrestrained quest for technological advancement affect, if not erode, human values. The school of thought argues that not everything in the world is rational or logical, and there needs to be a level of piety and spirituality related to religious beliefs and a level of emotion and empathy related to social equality and equity. In emerging economies, in particular, science and technology must be deployed to uplift the vast sections of the society. This requires a two-fold deployment of science and technology. At one level, the best of science and technology must be mastered to make India a globally competitive industrial power.

At another level, science and technology must be optimized to serve the vast indigent sections of the society through universal access to better social infrastructure and public services – roads, schools and colleges, hospitals, public transport, power, housing, for example. The former would bring in economic power while the latter would usher in social equity for India.

The New India is set for occupying centre-stage of global development from now on. It would not be merely in terms of the size of the national economy; rather, it would be in terms of India's talent contributing to global innovation and manufacturing. Over the last ten years or so, a massive effort has been made by the Narendra Modi Government to build on the past legacies of the 1960s, such as the IITs and space programs on one hand and bring India's competencies from Yoga to Science and Technology on to the global stage. There are determined government policies to leverage digital for all-round development and encourage innovation and manufacturing in cutting-edge fields. Ambitious programs of infrastructure building and self exploration have been drawn up. There is interest in understanding the centuries-old native sciences of India such as Ayurveda. This push for scientific temper with a humanistic touch must go on.

Chapter 12

New Generation Technological Education at the IITs

Optimal Track, Rather Than Fast-Track?

The Indian Institutes of Technology (IITs), India's central government owned premier institutions of national importance for technological education have been the Indian icons of globally competitive technical education. The initiatives they take, and the reforms they usher in, have a ripple effect in the entire field of technical education in India. The proposal that IITs should go in for fast-track engineering (B Tech) degree based on accelerated credits (in three and half years instead of four years) had the potential to churn the technical education scenario in India. This proposal must be viewed in the perspective that not several years ago, engineering degree in India required five years of full-time study. Had this proposal of three and half years become real, India would have been probably the first major country, after the USA, to provide a bachelor's degree in engineering in such a compressed time frame.

IITs are known to be cradles of high-pressure, high-performance education. The entry into IITs is itself a resultant of highly competitive Joint Entrance Examination (JEE) system, for which schoolboys start preparing years ahead through high intensity coaching. Given this context, an emphasis on credits for a compressed time frame could be adding to the high pressure robotized study system in the IITs, making students vulnerable to the risks and dangers of intense competitiveness. If other competitive institutions like National Institutes of Technology

(NITs) and other key universities follow suit, it could be a larger, national phenomenon of 'race to degree'. Another worry would be that other regional universities and colleges may try to follow suit and given the reduced level of study and examination solidity in such universities and colleges there could be a dilution of study standards in such institutions. At the same time, there also seem to be certain higher order goals in the proposed change which are yet to catch the attention. This chapter discusses the proposal for the IITs in the totality, and options, although the proposal has been abandoned. Figure 12.1 illustrates the challenges regarding the fast-track engineering degree proposal.

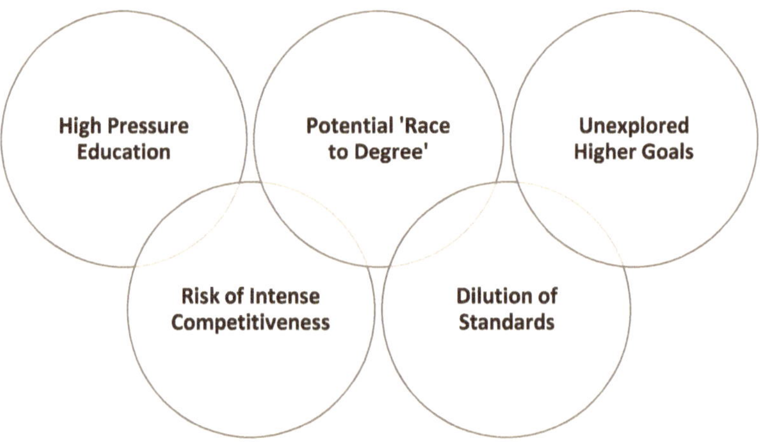

Figure 12.1: Challenges Regarding IITs' Fast-Track Engineering Degree Proposal

Flexibility

The IITs' proposal was announced by Partha Pratim Chakrabarti, the Director of IIT Kharagpur at the 60th convocation of the Institute on July 26, 2014. It is good that the proposal has not become a reality, for the implications are many. Professor Chakrabarti's proposal had an important concept of flexibility. The fast-track option was proposed to be essentially for those students who could accrue the requisite credits. The proposal also provided for a more languid pace, extending up to 8 years for the 'slow learners.' The fast-track option envisaged that the 'saved' six months could be utilized for job or entrepreneurship. It also allowed inter-IIT portability of credits to utilize the centres of excellence that exist in various IITs. With these features in tow, the fast-track proposal would appear more holistic. This, does not, however take the focus away from the weighty nature of a true technological curriculum and whether adequate justice is being done to it under even a four-year program. The pitfall in any credit-based system is the equation of credit to learning and subjects to knowledge, all of which require certain minimum periods of time for attention, absorption, and assimilation.

The undergraduate level engineering programs are both foundational and specialist in nature. Despite the proliferation of various engineering streams, each engineer irrespective of the specialization must be well versed in certain core engineering studies. These relate to mathematics, sciences, humanities, design and drawing principles, and a foundation of each of the core or basic engineering specializations like civil, mechanical, electrical, electronics and computers and each of these must have a corresponding laboratory practice, which should expose the students to a wide range of machining, forming, casting, welding, and bonding practices related to various kinds of materials. Similar are the requirements in other engineering disciplines. Given the heavy knowledge and practice load on the one hand, and the extremes of extracurricular pulls and social media distractions on the other hand, the case seems to be more for extension, rather than compression, of degree granting period.

Flights away

One question to ask is to whose benefit the acceleration would be if the fast-track graduate were to choose a job or another degree instead of the well-intended entrepreneurship. As we are aware, many of the IIT graduates end up taking up management diplomas in the equally reputed Indian Institutes of Management (IIMs) or go abroad for higher education or research. In the IIT Kharagpur convocation, Bharat Ratna Professor C N R Rao exhorted the IITians to stay in the country and contribute to India's scientific and technological capital, citing his own example of success. If the fast-track graduates see the credit-based graduation as an opportunity to explore other options elsewhere, the basis of advancing gets called into question. A total credit score of 182 in 7 semesters, covering theory, laboratory, workshop, and fieldwork, as proposed, is an intensely packed study and learning schedule (a typical course take 190 credits over 10 semesters). Besides the IITs, other leading institutes offer dual degree programs as well under a compressed time frame, relative to a traditional graduate plus postgraduate combination.

By the same token, allowing a highly relaxed period for course completion may also be misplaced. Given that all entrants to the IITs are competent and competitive, allowing a level of extended flexibility would be a loss in the formation of intellectual capital in India. Considering that certain students do find the pressure a trifle too much, flexibility for completing the course up to 6 years could be more in order. Also, extending inter-IIT portability to cover at least one year of residence could expose the students to not only other centres of excellence but even to other residential cultures as well. Given that the new program has never been rolled out (it was, in fact, proposed for implementation from the academic year 2016-17, and in a phased manner!), there is an opportunity to reinforce the good points of the fast-track program (in fact, it should be called optimal track program!), overcome the weaknesses and develop a techno-entrepreneurial ecosystem that maximizes the benefits of the proposal.

Specializations

The key to success of a flexible credit-based system is the availability of several specializations and micro-specializations on one hand and well-coordinated academic planning. Providing total flexibility to the student in course choice could lead to diffused learning while too much control could lead to the defeat of the system itself. It is important that the academic deans of the IITs develop a course planner which explains why a cluster of related specializations would make a holistic sense compared to a random choice of courses. The course credits must be hierarchically defined based on complexity and relational synergy of the courses. It may be a good idea for the IITs to develop an App exclusively for course and credit planning under the fast-track system. The App must also link specializations offered by the various IITs to define a total universe of specializations. There could be certain thorny issues related to different IITs providing differential values to similar specializations based on the excellence they think they possess in the domain. This will be one challenge of flexibility.

The other challenge will be providing the specializations themselves. For a mechanical engineering stream, the range of main and specialization courses can range from thermodynamics to robotics. Whether a robotics specialization could be common for mechanical and electronics mainstreams, or whether it would need to be customized to each mainstream would be one call. Given the fast-paced developments, what would be the life of a course (say, 3 or 5 years) would be another call. Whether courses that belong to a graduate level (for example, prosthetics) would be a good fit for an undergraduate level mechanical engineering course could be another call. Whether specializations should be only subject matter or whether even laboratory or workshop practice could qualify as specializations is yet another call. Ideally, specializations should have a range that plays on one's aptitude for further academic specialization or industrial practice. The challenges are likely to be more in domains where product lifecycles are getting shorter. One way would be to link up academic expertise, research directions, consulting practice and industrial inputs in development of state-of-the-art specializations. Figure 12.2 summarises the key success factors for flexible credit-based systems.

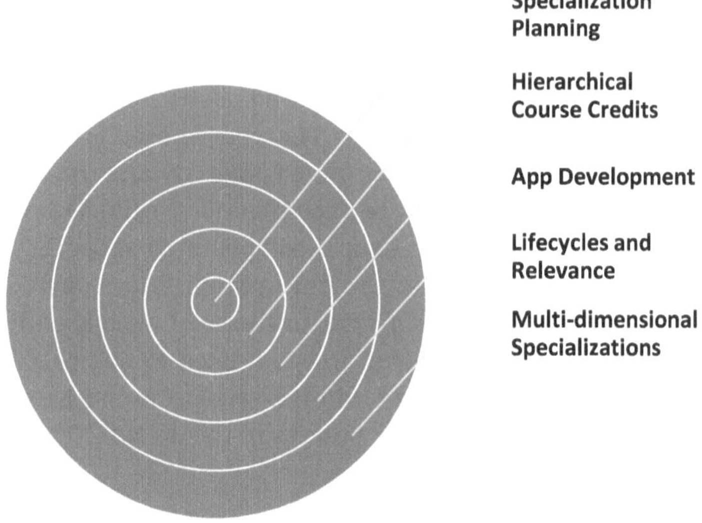

Figure 12.2: Key Success Factors for Flexible Credit-Based Systems

Entrepreneurship in IITs

Given that an important aspect of the fast-track proposal is to release one semester for entrepreneurial activity, availability of an entrepreneurial ecosystem within the IIT system, or otherwise, would be a prerequisite. A few IITs, notably IIT Madras, IIT Bombay, IIT Kharagpur, and IIT (BHU) Varanasi have experimented with creating entrepreneurial ecosystems as adjuncts to their educational systems. IIT Madras has set up IIT Madras Incubation Cell. IIT Bombay has set up Society for Innovation and Entrepreneurship. IIT (BHU) has established Malaviya Centre for Innovation, Incubation and Entrepreneurship. Each of these has incorporated specific initiatives funded by the IITs, Central Ministries or IIT alumni themselves. Even a newer IIT like IIT Hyderabad has set up E-Cell for entrepreneurs. Some of these have been in operation since 1999, and important major entrepreneurial startups in electric vehicles and spacecraft emerged from these incubation initiatives. Even though IITM has provided physical infrastructure through IIT

Madras Research Park adjacent to IITM campus, it appears that large companies began to take space in the Park, impacting the space that could be otherwise offered for startups.

Undoubtedly, the strong technological foundations at IITs, and the personality strengths of the IITians make them look at entrepreneurship as a career option more confidently, the only inhibiting factor being the hugely attractive job opportunities they automatically command. That said, convergence of futuristic research with foundational technology, and combination of financial support with commercial insights would be necessary to create an ecosystem that would make entrepreneurship widespread across IITs. Special emphasis should be laid on socially relevant low cost, high technology products. Entrepreneurship, however, requires more than a feasible product idea. Recent research suggests that an entrepreneur with a product idea needs a core organization of likeminded passionate friends to make a success of entrepreneurship. Even some of the biggest globalized startups of today such as Apple, Amazon, eBay, Facebook, Salesforce.com as well as regional startups like Project A Ventures, Eyeota, Flipkart, RedBus validate this thesis.

Indigenous ecosystem

The other aspect is that successful entrepreneurship needs certain other skills in addition to wholly technical skills. This has prompted the Hyderabad based management school, the Indian School of Business (ISB) to launch, as a two-year programme at ISB, Technology Entrepreneurship Programme to equip select engineering students with skills to become entrepreneurs. Microsoft Ventures, Google, and a few other global corporations are supporting the programme. The larger question still would be whether even a broader educational curriculum for entrepreneurship or cross-collaboration between IITs (and/or NITs) and IIMs (and/or ISB) would be completely sufficient. The philosophical question is also whether entrepreneurship can only arise from premier institutes or could emerge as a broader national phenomenon. Prima facie, creative technological ideas ought to emerge from any institute which has higher technological and research competencies. Idea incubation (example, IIT Madras Incubation Cell) and licensing of patentable ideas (yet to happen in a big way) from institutes of higher technology is one facet of creation of a broader national entrepreneurship ecosystem.

The real answer could lie in restoring and rejuvenating the traditional economic employment system of India which was rooted in skill- and craft-based self-employment system but has faced dilution due to the attraction of readymade and assured career options that could arise from formal educational qualifications. It is, therefore, gratifying that some of the IIT entrepreneurship schools are focusing on socially relevant product or service ideas (example, Centre for Social Entrepreneurship and Innovation at IIT Madras). Real developments that can be commercialized would need to focus on market applications rather than technology roots. For example, could a variable speed micro-motor be developed that could make a potter's work more productive, more consistent and of higher quality? Can a portable ultrasound linked with tablet computer be designed to take ultrasound diagnostics into the rural areas? Can there be a sanitizing solution for dry leaf plates (used extensively in certain southern states) to obviate the need for paper plates? Can solar panels, inverters and electricity power be integrated to reduce generated power consumptions? Can there be water purifying technology which does not waste any water? The optimal track for IITs could be in not fast-tracking credits per se, but in integrating latent market needs with creative technologies.

Chapter 13

Indian Institutes of Vocational Management (IIVMS)

Institutes for Next Generation Management

My first brush with management studies was in 1970 when I took an optional course of production management as part of my final year mechanical engineering course at Government College of Engineering, Anantapur, affiliated to Sri Venkateswara University, Tirupati. Thereafter, I had the opportunity to complete postgraduate and doctoral programs in industrial engineering and industrial management at the Indian Institute of Technology Madras, Chennai. Over the last 53 plus years, I kept in touch with the management disciplines as taught and as practised. As an engineer who pursued management studies, I was variously intrigued, fascinated, and circumspect, time to time, about the glamorous attraction of the management studies that tempted several thousands of engineers to branch off into management. The emergence of premium schools of business such as the Indian Institutes of Management (IIMs) only fuelled the trend. The more established premium schools of engineering, technology, and science such as the Indian Institutes of Technology (IITs) had to follow suit by establishing their own in-house departments or schools of business.

Unlike engineering, management studies have remained largely static over the last four decades. While more nuances may have come about, and while other disciplines such as mathematics, statistics, economics, sociology, psychology, and information technology may have enriched management, there have been no new disciplines that have emerged out of management.

Even Porter's theories of competitive strategy and competitive advantage (of the 1980s) made for compelling reading but elusive application. Overall, over the last five decades management studies helped graduates improve their conceptual, analytical and communication skills and leapfrog in their careers, leveraging their institutional moorings. With mushrooming of management studies and the increasing need for companies to secure operational advantage rather than strategic advantage, management studies need to move from the (now threatened) vantage position of prescriptive studies to a (future secure) position that would be more value generating and value sustaining. This chapter discusses a few options, some merely extensional and some truly transformational.

Art, science, skill

For too long, the debate on management focused on whether it is an art or science, the former view because of the strong people element in management and the latter view because of the strong quantitative element inherent in performance. Neither is wholly right or wrong but what is more relevant is that management needs to be like anything else - a profession of skill. There is an oft repeated criticism that the Indian educational system focuses too much on information and theory and too little on knowledge and application. As a result, there is a strident view that the workforce is qualified but not knowledgeable and where it is knowledgeable it is not skilled. One of the concerns on 'Make in India' reaching its full potential relates to the skill deficit arising out of the Indian educational system. Prime Minister Narendra Modi's very first exhortation has, therefore, been that India must focus on 3 S's of skill, scale and speed. On these, a common view could be that individual efforts are required for skill development and management efforts are needed to achieve scale and speed. In a distorted view of this, managers tend to believe that only the employees at the bottom of the organizational pyramid need to be skilled while the higher levels need to be only well versed in managerial processes and focused on others' outcomes than on their own contributions.

Historically, organizations have looked at skill only from a workman perspective and even categorized workmen as unskilled, semi-skilled, skilled, and highly skilled. The fact of the matter is that everyone needs to be skilled, whether one is a material handler, forklift operator or machinist. It is only that different types of skills are required for different roles. As understood from serious incidents of quality, compliance or safety, lack of skill even at the lowest levels can cause serious dislocations or disruptions. Given this perspective, it would be an even greater organizational distortion to conceptualize that skills are required at frontline levels and higher levels need only capabilities of management and leadership, classified as art or science. Management and leadership must move out of the exotic domains of visioning, strategizing and performance management and concentrate equally on individual contributions that are commensurately and consummately skilled. The synergistic arithmetic of organizations has two components; individual and team based. Managers and leaders are also governed by similar value arithmetic. There are two approaches to achieve this in a phased manner. The first is by redefining management curricula. The second is by making management studies completely vocational, and skill based. Figure 13.1 shows ways to enhance skill development in organizations.

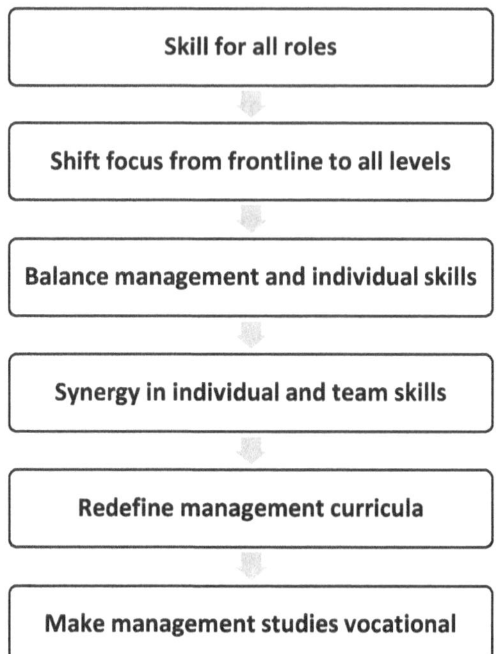

Figure 13.1: Enhancing Skill Development in Organizations

Specialization and customization

A logical way forward is to increase the extent of specialization and customization. Specializations such as production, operations, marketing, finance, human resources etc., have always been there. The next frontiers of specialization must be three dimensional. The first dimension must be on specific industry orientation. There is no point in letting management studies remain generic and prescriptive. The least that can be done is to customize studies to industries, which will retain the basic scientific and technological foundations of one's professional undergraduate studies. One may envisage at least 50 such industry specializations to start with. The second dimension must be on converting themes into subjects. Fashionable topics such as visioning, integration, diversification, costing, execution, self-realization, and self-actualization which are nothing more than sections or chapters currently must be developed into holistic subjects. The third dimension must be on focusing on management for differentiated national cultures. Setting up and running industries or businesses could be significantly different across nations, and customization would help in making management graduates better.

The above is based on the requirement that management studies must not remain as generic studies as they now are. Two years is a long time in one's educational career, especially as one gets closer to the career doorstep. By remaining generic, management studies not only make students unlearn their hard-learnt technical competencies but also make them managers of others' competencies rather than contributors of their own intellectual might. Today's generation can learn from diverse sources from the childhood days and it does not require a management capstone course to acquire soft skills. In fact, soft skills, including conceptual, analytical and communication skills, must be integrated from the basic school curricula stage. Management courses by becoming more specialized and customized will become more relevant to the industry. Possibly, educational institutions would be averse to such specialization as there could be uncertainty in securing high student intake. Specialized and customized management courses, not unnaturally, would require early career planning by the students (and their families who have a say over the career choices of students in the Indian context!).

Indian Institutes of Vocational Management (IIVMs)

Vocational courses are those that are directly deployable onto a work situation by teaching and developing work related skills. Industrial Training Institutes (ITIs) with their technician courses are typical providers of vocational studies. Even at a higher level, with reference to scientific and engineering studies, it is commonly understood in all engineering institutions that while classroom teaching is essential and inevitable science is best learnt in laboratories and technology is best appreciated in workshops. Classroom education is also embedded with problem solving to illustrate and imbibe the theoretical principles. In contrast, management studies, despite the gallant efforts to bring in the case study approach and occasional industry guest lectures, remain theoretical and classroom laden. In addition, the inevitability of reducing complex real-world issues to manageable assignments leaves the students quite distanced from the complex realities. Added to this, the convenient management principle of holding someone else accountable and responsible for elemental projects makes management studies even more superficial. The earlier recommended approach of specialization and customization in subjects, industries and cultures is the first foundational step to make management vocational.

To institutionalize vocational management studies, it would be necessary to establish a string of Indian Institutes of Vocational Management (IIVMs). The existing management institutes may be given options to convert themselves into IIVMs or establish adjunct IIVMs. As illustrated in Figure 13.2, vocational management studies must have five essential components. The first is that an equal distribution of pedagogy between classroom and workplace must prevail. If it is a one-year program, six months must be in classroom and six months in a workplace, and in the case of a two-year program, one year each in classroom and workplace. The second is that project work is not a surrogate for real time work experience. If there exist 12 courses in the theoretical curriculum, there must be 12 projects, each reflecting the main theme of each of the subjects. The third is that the faculty must comprise an equal number of fulltime academic faculty and visiting workplace managers and leaders. The fourth is that the curriculum should be managed, and students' performance evaluated by an academic board of both in-house faculty and industry experts. The fifth is that the vocational management institutes should run off-campus management programs aggressively on the lines of Birla Institute of Technology & Science (BITS), Pilani. These five principles can transform the way management courses are conceptualized and run as truly application oriented vocational programs. This, of course, requires close collaboration between industries and IIVMs. The exciting opportunity of next generation management - vocational management - is well worth the effort to overcome the challenges of collaboration.

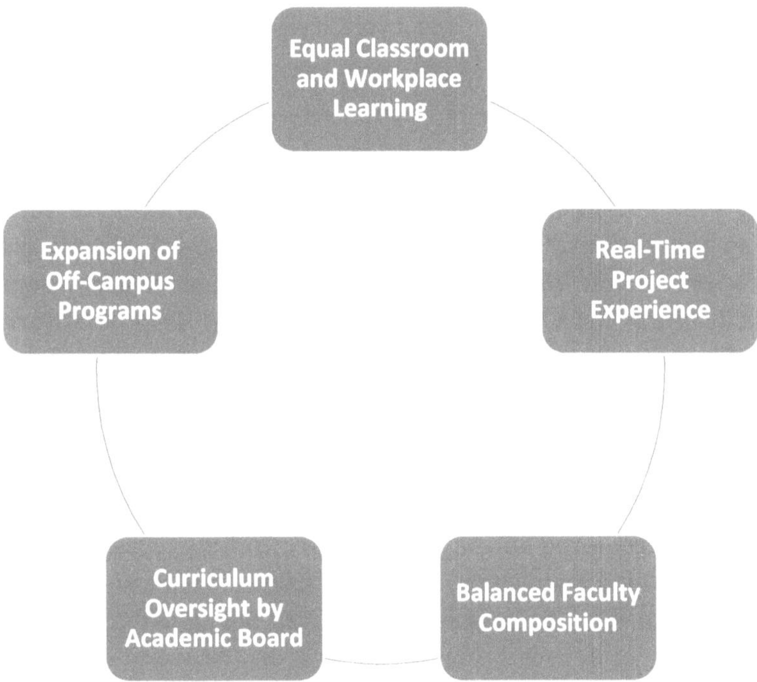

Figure 13.2: Five Essential Components of Vocational Management Studies

Chapter 14

Global Education for Global Leaders

A New Bilateral Paradigm Towards 2030

Dr Marshall Goldsmith, one of the top CEO coaches of the world and the author of several bestsellers on leadership delivered a speech at the National HRD Network's silver jubilee event. Addressing the CXOs, he made a point that despite cultural differences across countries, the CEOs of multi-billion-dollar companies have a lot in common. Amongst such common characteristics, he mentioned Western education as an important feature even if they went to school in India. He also said that a future CEO should have five things that were not required in the past: global thinking, cross-cultural appreciation, tech-savvy, building partnerships and shared leadership. Though he was candid about the egoistic and other problems of leaders, his insistence on Western education seemed like his quick fix for global thinking, one of his five leadership ingredients.

To interpret Dr Goldsmith's comments in a perspective, it could be that he views Western education as a surrogate for some of the important attributes of the Western (the US, for simplicity) educational system. These could relate to a graded educational experience that emphasizes logic, openness, boldness, expressiveness and experimentation, and benefits from superior laboratory and other facilities. These contrast with the Asian (Indian, for simplicity) educational experience that supports tradition, caution, deference, and conformity, and suffers from constraints of campus infrastructure. Western educational system focuses on expressive, at times even overwhelming, competitiveness in everyday life as opposed to the Indian educational system that emphasizes competitiveness more in examination routines, and accommodation in day-to-day routines. Western culture promotes inter-personal independence of the individual with dependence on one's head while oriental culture promotes interpersonal dependence of the individual with dependence on one's heart.

Flood and trickle

American education continues to be the first choice for higher education for Indian students and parents, whether they have a strong materialistic mind or a strong nationalistic heart. As a result, the number of Indian students applying for US student visas has been growing exponentially. In FY2022, there was a significant surge in the issuance of student visas in India, marking an increase of more than 43 percent compared to FY2021. With over 115,000 F-1 visas granted to Indian students during that fiscal year, India has now positioned itself as a strong contender to surpass China, which had 61,894 student visas issued, and potentially become the leading source country for total international students in the United States. Together, China and India contribute to nearly 50 percent of US student visas. The question, however, is whether the students prefer the US educational system for higher education for the sheer educational experience for global leadership or to pursue an American dream of a career in a superior ecosystem. While both could be viable reasons, probably not many are so futuristic as to pursue American education as a global leadership qualification. Figure 14.1 summarises the Indian students' preferences for American education.

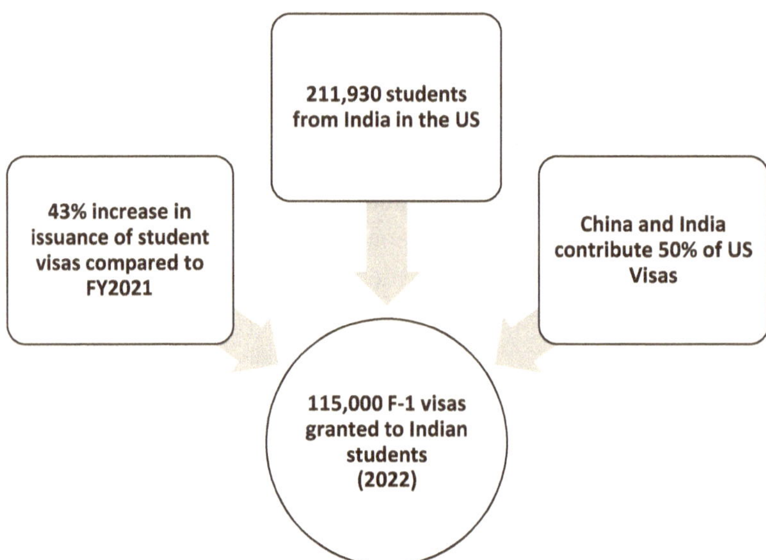

Figure 14.1: Indian Students' Preferences for American Education

For the few who have become the CEOs or CXOs of multi-billion multinational corporations such as Indira Nooyi (Pepsico), Satya Nadella (Microsoft), Ajay Banga (World Bank Group), Shantanu Narayen (Adobe), Vikram Pandit (The Orogen Group), Arvind Krishna (IBM) Sundar Pichai (Google), Nikesh Arora(Palo Alto Networks) and Ajit Jain (Berkshire Hathaway), the reason is not necessarily the Western education as several had higher education in India too. Various others have occupied leadership positions in Indian multinationals without any Western degrees. While Bloomberg commented that Indian cultural ethos of empathy, humility, patience, emotional bonding, and passion for growth as a reason for Indians becoming CEOs in global MNCs, it is also clear that out of the flood of Indians seeking US higher education only a trickle makes it to the top. This leads us to wonder on the validity of Dr Goldsmith's prescription of Western education as an essential prerequisite for future global leaders. In likely fact of the future, there could, on the other hand, be a dramatic shift in favour of Asian education and experience.

Asian resurgence 2030

According to research reports, India is projected to become the World's third largest economy by 2028, With India's GDP surpassing that of Germany and the UK. India's nominal GDP is forecast to rise from USD 3.75 trillion in 2023 to USD 6 trillion by 2027, resulting in a larger GDP than Japan and the largest Western European economies of Germany, France, and the UK. GDP growth rates in Q3 and Q4 of FY24 are around 8 percent, higher than the growth rates experienced in Q1 and Q2 of FY24. As a result, India's GDP growth is expected to be beyond 6.5 per cent in FY24.

Today's challenges of the emerging economies in terms of deficient urban and rural infrastructure, underdeveloped transportation services, inadequate power and energy, increasing population, poor healthcare, and sanitation, and so many other shortfalls would be great opportunities of tomorrow, calling for massive investment in infrastructure development and economic growth. A qualifying requirement for this transformation would be the importance attached to organic technological innovation. India's Mars mission (Mangalyaan) that has successfully placed India's satellite in the orbit of Mars in the very first attempt in 2014 at a cost lower than the cost of a Hollywood blockbuster movie (a point eloquently made by India's Prime Minister Narendra Modi in his Madison Square, New York address) illustrated that Indian engineering and scientific talent can achieve technological self-reliance even in the most sophisticated fields, with a structured mission and progressive leadership. The lunar mission Chandrayaan - 3 which landed successfully on the Moon in August 2023 made India as the first and only nation to land a Rover on the South Pole of the Moon. This is followed by India's first solar mission, Aditya-L1. Indian Scientific Research Organization (ISRO), a Government of India body has certainly shown the way for a techno-savvy India.

Factors and markets

Eventually, global economic development would seek a global equilibrium, driven by differential factor advantages and differential market sizes. Like water flows from a higher plane to a lower plane and heat transfers from a higher temperature heat sink to a lower temperature heat sink, technologies and finances would flow to economies where they can be best utilized. Global developmental equilibrium would need to happen, even if it were to take years and decades. In this process, leadership is a critical driver of how to access and deploy resources, be it finance, people and machines, or naturally occurring resources like oil, gas, water, wind, minerals, metals, and any other element. Leadership is also a critical ingredient of understanding various local markets, developing customized products and services, and integrating with local consumer needs. If these are the imperatives, leadership must understand local factor endowments and local market needs and explore how multi-national resources can be networked to synergize each local economy.

It goes to the credit of global Fast Moving Consumer Goods (FMCG) companies that they ventured into underdeveloped markets decades ago despite several challenges and uncertainties and, in the process, secured a place in such countries that is on par with indigenous companies. As the underdeveloped economies moved on to become developing economies a few years ago, and now emerging economies with potential to become fully developed over the next two decades, the pioneering FMCG companies have discovered that their venturesome strategies fuelled sustainable global growth for them. Companies such as Unilever, Colgate-Palmolive, Proctor & Gamble, Gillette, GSK Consumer, Microsoft, Pepsi, CocaCola, Henkel and Reckitt Benckiser come to mind. In other fields as well, companies such as Suzuki, GE, Siemens, ABB, Nokia, Philips, Cummins, and Alstom have taken early roots. All such successful companies viewed India as an important market and supply source but some like Unilever have seen India as a select leadership talent source for their global needs.

A new bilateral paradigm

As India and China match the highly developed economies by value in a few years from now, global corporations must develop a significantly different paradigm for nurturing global leaders. The conventional models that local leaders must be Western educated to have global acceptance (typical Goldsmith type prescription) or that expat leaders must spend a few years each in several emerging countries (typical global automobile industry's practice) would be found wanting when India and China (as well as other emerging market economies) race at full economic throttle. Fundamentally, future global leaders would be developed with specific collaborating countries in mind. Such combinations could be US and India or US and China, Japan and India or Korea and India, UK and India or UK and China, India and China or India and Brazil, and so on. The Western origin person who would have graduate education of the West would be immersed in postgraduate education of the East while the Eastern origin person who would have graduate education of the East would be immersed in postgraduate education of the West.

Put differently, the new global leader would not rest content with viewing education as imparting only professional knowledge or leading to a different employment opportunity. Education would be seen as an immersive cultural experience of a different nation with a style of pedagogy and a community of co-learners and co-executors unique to that national culture. As much as an Indian student with US employment aspiration would like a US higher education so must a US student with the aspiration of becoming an India-centric leader take to Indian higher education. Ahead of this paradigm being a part of mainstream general education, executive education could be the right vehicle to develop the new generation of focused global leaders. Executives should be encouraged to take up fulltime residential higher education courses in diverse emerging market countries on sabbatical depending on the global growth orientation of the companies. For the new bilateral global education paradigm to be effective, educational institutions in India and China (and other emerging nations) must elevate their campus ecosystems, learning communities and curricula to integrate the best of locally embedded and intrinsic culture, knowledge and practice with globally applicable professional knowledge, tools, and techniques. Figure 14.2 shows the ways to develop a new generation of focused global leaders.

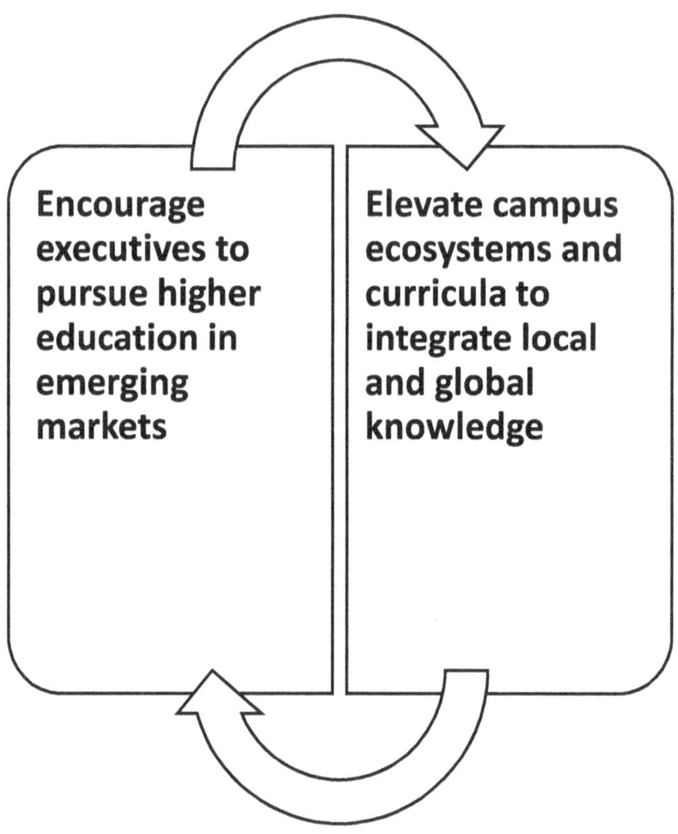

Figure 14.2: Ways to Develop New Generation of Focused Global Leaders

Enterprise Perspectives

Chapter 15

Continuing Education for Employees

Consistent Strength for Organizations

Two things never stand still in life; the first, of course, is time, and the second, less recognized, is knowledge. Knowledge gained through education is commonly seen as the prime ticket for career entry. Consummate application of such formal knowledge as well as experiential knowledge gained in one's career is the key to further progress in career and life. Industrial and business organizations are paradoxical. At one level, they are at the leading edge of technology. At another level, they tend to stagnate at past levels of knowledge. This is attributed mainly to employees being engaged in repetitive jobs and not being challenged to be at contemporary standards of knowledge. A study of different companies reveals that those companies which invest in continuing education for their employees tend to be more competitive.

Continuing education even in the best of companies is a misnomer. Usually, it is limited to providing "canned programmes" to a proportion of employees, "allowing" a few employees to pursue formal part-time degree or higher degree programmes, and "sponsoring" even fewer to executive development programmes. Some companies avoid all of these on the basis that there is no substitute for on-the-job-training on a continuing basis. These policies cause a stagnation of skill levels and lead to competitive decline. In some cases, companies which are impacted by competitive decline engage multiple external consultants at great costs to reinvent themselves. In contrast to such uncoordinated efforts, it would be more appropriate to embed continuous learning in organisational culture, with emphasis on contemporaneity and quality.

Shared responsibility

Continuing education is a shared responsibility of both the company and employees. While the company has a lead responsibility in articulating that it places a premium on knowledge, and following it up with a learning environment, employees need to consider continuing education as their responsibility too. In fact, continuing education is a very useful platform to align the career possibilities that a company can offer and the career expectations that an employee has. Continuing education helps a company in that it could derive greater competitiveness through skilled-up employees and be able to offer them better opportunities. For employees it is an opportunity to offer a superior or different value proposition to the company and seek career progression in the same or different track.

The extent to which responsibility for continuing education is felt by company and employees varies based on the business context. Start-ups, by definition, are innovative and, where required, learn by experimentation; they are likely to have little penchant for formal continuing education. Growing firms evidently are competitive and successful but also cost conscious; they are likely to adopt a need-based approach for continuing formal education. Mature firms are engaged in defensive strategies and are likely to be open to a skill-based approach for continuing education. Declining firms are engaged in survival strategies and are likely to have little time for continuing education. While employees may like to prefer a degree or skill-based approach, the company context determines their approach. Companies of all types must eschew such limiting assumptions and institutionalize continuing formal education for the employees.

Multiple approaches

Companies could adopt three approaches in fulfilling their share of responsibility. The first is a 'qualification gap' based approach. In this approach, the company determines an optimal qualification for each role (as contrasted with the minimal qualification required for entry) and encourages acquisition of degrees or certifications/accreditations for bridging the gap. The second is a 'competitiveness gap' based approach. In this approach, the company maps people competencies to company's competitiveness and does whatever is required to make the company competitive. The third is an 'industry leadership' approach. In this approach, the company believes in a heady mix of superlative qualifications and competitive competencies for a highly differentiated performance. While most companies would follow the first or second approach, top ranking consulting firms, law firms and investment banking firms appear to be following the third approach. Figure 15.1 illustrates the three approaches to fulfilling corporate responsibility for continuing education.

Figure 15.1: Approaches to Fulfilling Corporate Responsibility for Continuing Education

Employees' approach to continuing education, by and large, depends on the nature of the company. A technology and research-intensive industry will require skills that are typically offered in leading educational institutions. Skills required for other industries may be more easily sourced in the general marketplace. Regardless, in general the approach tends to favour the acquisition of higher formal degrees. Whether employees do it through part time education or by taking a break depends on personal circumstances, company environment as well as career shift that is desired. Research indicates that employees do not consider in-house training as being supportive of career aspirations; they also consider external short-term courses as little more than of marginal support for either on the job performance or career shift.

Education as mind-set

The primary objective of industries and businesses is to provide products and services, and not to educate. Similarly, the primary objective of industrial and business employees is to put their knowledge to use. To conceive, therefore, of a situation where industries and businesses as well as employees focus only on education is somewhat impractical. However, the need for continuing education as brought out above is critical. This chapter suggests a few mind-set approaches to accomplish the objectives.

Continuous as lifelong

The first is to consider continuous as really meaning lifelong. As a concept, continuous education has lesser emotional connectivity to an individual than lifelong education. Once an individual gets into a mind-set that education is a lifelong, value adding process, he or she will surely develop ownership. Similarly, it focusses to the company that the continuous education initiative would need to be a part of life skill development of an employee. The concept of 'lifelong' is humbling as well as futuristic, for both employees and companies.

Company as campus

Companies take many structural approaches to supporting their versions of continuing education. These include setting up their own in-house technical training centres with pilot equipment for on-hands training and management development centres for development of executive and managerial skills. These, however, tend to be just a part of the company infrastructure and figure more as slots in training calendar. The compelling proposition, on the other hand, is to consider the company as a campus wherein every piece of equipment, every bit of procedure and every interaction with a person provides learning opportunities.

Individual as learner

While the company has a lead responsibility to provide a learning ecosystem, it is for and up to the individual to mould himself or herself as a perpetual learner. Being a learner does not make one a novice; only the insecure would feel that way. Being a learner and asking questions should never be seen as infra dig by employees or management. Wise scientists learn from every reaction of an experiment, wise operators from every rhythm of their equipment, and wise executives learn from every interaction they have in the company.

Learning processes

When we think of learning processes, things like classrooms, flip boards, audio-visuals, presentations, course materials etc., come to mind usually. Some think of off-site events and programmes as great learning opportunities. However, all these are at best accessories and aids to the learning processes. The real learning, that too perpetual learning, happens through the following personal approaches. Figure 15.2 illustrates the perpetual learning through personal approaches.

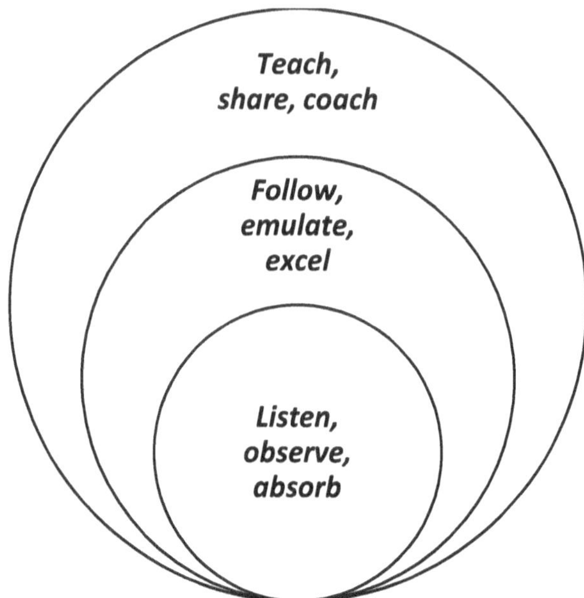

Figure 15.2: Perpetual Learning Through Personal Approaches

Listen, observe, absorb

In keeping with the prime responsibility on the individual to learn, the prime responsibility for learning approach also shall be that of the individual. It is fairly simple too. For a perfect learning process, the individual must listen intently, observe closely, and absorb earnestly. These processes must take place in all interactions, peer to peer or boss to subordinate. In several cases, there could be learning opportunities from the younger reporting staff too. Learning environment is usually an expressive and empowering environment.

Follow, emulate, excel

The objective of learning is to excel in performance. This is usually preceded by two fundamental stages of following and emulating. Following is the process of merely implementing the learnings as absorbed. It is task-oriented learning, putting into effect the 'know-how' learnt. Emulation is the process of thinking and acting like the person providing learning inputs; it is mastery of both 'know-how' and 'know-why'. Excelling is the process of creative thinking and execution based on the learnings imparted and/or received. Excelling is the result of empowered learning.

Teach, share, coach

Everyone has a responsibility to disseminate learnings as much as they absorb. This again occurs through a three-stage process. Most people who are well-versed in their art tend to teach. Those who teach prepare their learners only for 'know-how'. A few others not only teach but also share their thinking around the subject matter of interest. Such people help the learners absorb both the 'know-how' and 'know-why'. A few go beyond both the stages and truly coach the learners overcome their issues and limitations and become what they can truly become.

The winning twelve

This chapter has reviewed the ticker of continuing education that most organizations would like to carry and proposed that it should be considered more as lifelong education. It has reviewed current shared responsibilities between a company and its employees and noted that while a company has the lead responsibility to create a learning ecosystem the prime responsibility for learning must be that of an individual. It has considered the multiple approaches currently adopted and postulated that they serve to accessorize rather than elevate continuing education as a lifelong journey.

The chapter proposed twelve elements of a lifelong learning journey. On one plane is a true learning platform that embeds the concept of lifelong learning, with perpetually learning individuals considering the entire company as their learning campus. It also proposes an easy and feasible multi-step process to learn through listening, observing, and absorbing to be able to follow, emulate and eventually excel. It legislates that those with superior knowledge must endeavour to teach, share, and coach all the time. Lifelong learning is a humbling feeling and a rewarding experience. It is a win-win for both employees and organizations.

Chapter 16

National Competence Consistency

Key for Global Leadership through "Make in India"

There is perhaps no nation that has as much history of pioneering knowledge, dating back to several centuries, in eclectic sciences and technologies as India has. Yet, India has struggled to rediscover and fulfil the potential in recent past (despite some significant achievements in certain areas of industry and infrastructure as well as space technology). Prime Minister Narendra Modi's clarion call to global investors and global industries to "Make in India" resonates well with India as a resurgent nation that believes in self-reliance and global leadership. Modi has also rightly laid stress on skill development as the basis for building scale and scope in the manufacturing, research, and other areas. Though the national goal and the enabling strategic direction are well understood, the need for an almost revolutionary transformation in the competency paradigm is perhaps not fully understood. Successful nations on global missions have achieved such status based on making the required competencies a national comparative advantage. Figure 16.1 summarises the key factors that influence global manufacturing outsourcing.

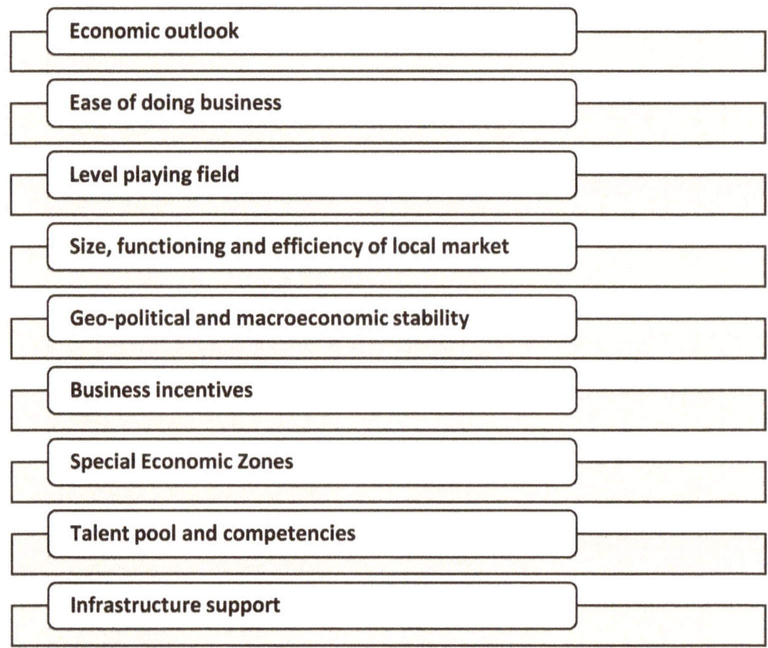

Figure 16.1: Factors Influencing Global Manufacturing Outsourcing

India's industrial development has been on fragmented lines as is well known. It is characterised by a few big capable firms with national competitive posture and several mid- and small-scale firms with regional or sub-regional presence. The former can develop or access and compete on technology while the latter struggle to access, let alone develop and compete on, technologies. This does not mean that a firm must be only big to be competent; as Japan and Korea illustrate, it is possible for even small and medium companies to be technologically competent. Many times, technological lag in India is attributed to scale related investments and finance; on the other hand, the lag is due to a managerial and leadership approach that fails to utilise all factors, especially technology, optimally. This lacuna needs to be addressed because global leadership can come about for India only when competencies are pan-Industrial and reflect a national characteristic of consistency. That India has some distance to go on this aspect is illustrated by the following example.

Unreasonable Spread

Airline industry is one of the most technology-, people- and logistics- intensive industries globally. It is also one of the most capital-intensive industries. Despite this shared industry characteristic, different firms in the industry display different levels of performance. In India, most of the leading airlines have invested in a fleet of modern planes, and the associated piloting, crew, ground handling, maintenance, and ticketing infrastructure. Yet, the way the individual airlines utilise their respective infrastructure and organisation to deliver the ultimate services is paradoxical. This is because, despite the core need for customer centricity, different companies come up differently on important parameters such as on-time performance, value for money, in-flight entertainment, in-flight food/beverages, cabin crew, landing/take-off, check-in, baggage delivery, cabin maintenance, seat comfort/leg room, website, and overall experience. Given the sophisticated nature of the airline industry, one would expect the airlines to uniformly meet certain base metrics. This demonstrates that customer centricity is a core competency that firms in the airlines industry must possess.

Some surveys of airlines pointed to a huge variation in performance as perceived by travellers (as captured through a survey by a leading travel agency a few years ago). For example, with reference to on-time performance the approval ratings ranged from a measly 0.4 percent to a respectable 69.6 percent. Except two airlines (the second trailing at 16.3 percent), all the others had a very low range of 0.4 percent to 6.3 percent on this factor. In fact, on each of the other eleven parameters too, the spread has been inordinately high. In terms of overall experience, the pecking order has been 42.0 percent, 37.8 percent, 10.6 percent, 5.5 percent, 2.0 percent, 1.0 percent and 1.0 percent.

Even more tellingly, on safety too, the approval ratings showed a dangerously wide range from 0.8 percent to 31.2 percent, with only 14.9 percent of the respondents deeming all the airlines to be equally safe. Clearly, same, or similar assets and talent base has been resulting in radically different perceptions of performance. If the survey brings out one factor as a common theme, it is the lack of consistency in competence as reflected in performance delivery and user experience. Core competency emerges from possession of knowledge and consistent application.

Defining Competency

Core Competency is a concept introduced by C K Prahalad and Gary Hamel in strategic management theory. Core competency is defined by them as a harmonized combination of multiple resources and skills that distinguish a firm in the marketplace. As illustrated in Figure 16.2, core competencies must fulfil three critical criteria: (i) provide potential access to a wide variety of markets, (ii) should make a significant contribution to the perceived customer benefits of the end-product, and (iii) be difficult to imitate by competitors.

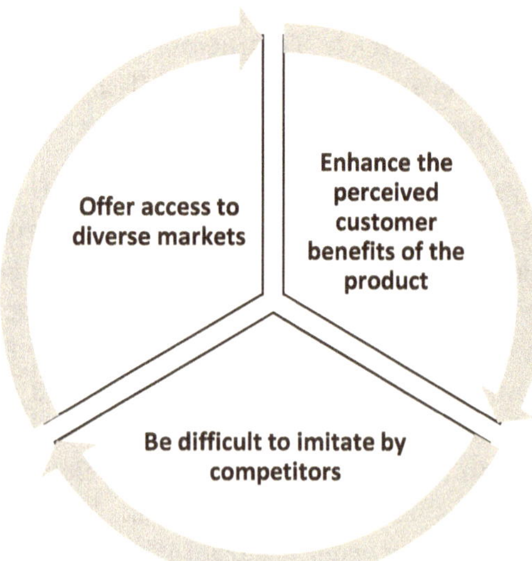

Figure 16.2: Three Critical Criteria for Core Competencies

Examples are OLED screens by Samsung, camera sensors and lenses by Sony, sound systems by Dolby, and so on. A company can have multiple core competencies. The more the number of firms in an industry with core competencies, and the more the number of such industries in a nation, the nation can then have sustainable competitive advantage.

Generally, the route to gaining core competency is seen to be through innovative design, quality embedded manufacture and value-based pricing, all carried out with customer needs in mind. At the same time, core competency is larger and broader than technological innovation, advanced manufacturing, or cost leadership. Even when technology is commoditised a company could have core competency through innovative deployment of technology. Even if the machining lines are common to different firms, core competency can be achieved through delivered quality and efficiency. Similarly, seemingly similar products can be delivered in unique ways by firms. It could be different from direct product or manufacturing. It could be an underlying technological platform that powers everything that a firm does, for example, digital. It could also be different from even technology. A company's core competency could be its ability to simply blend multiple things, known or unknown in any mix, into a unique product, service or process that is distinctive to the company.

National Consistency

If a nation must qualify as the world's destination for any competitive activity it must first qualify as a consistently competent nation for that activity. India has been able to do that in the field of information technology. From the established metro cities to the emerging urban regions, aptitude and skill sets for information technology became available, making computer coding and system architecture a nationally consistent competency. In respect of manufacturing, India has been able to develop certain self-reliance in heavy engineering from independence. However, diversified manufacture and global competitiveness were eluding due to restrictive and inward-looking government policies. Post-liberalization in 1992, regional and/or product-wise clusters of competencies began developing. Notable among these are the clusters for automobiles, auto components, steel making, shipbuilding, defence equipment, heavy engineering, pharmaceuticals, jewels, watches, movies, collieries, and a few other sectors. On the other hand, in respect of certain industries the competencies have been just firm-specific and not even region-specific. However, from 2014, there has been a determined bid for Make in India covering all established and emerging industries, which is paying off.

National or regional consistency has, to-date, been a resultant of top-down initiatives. The establishment of heavy engineering and steel companies in public sector and the other noted companies in public/private sectors created a pull factor for the generation of competencies in the 1950s and 1960s. Initial training by overseas collaborators followed by indigenisation of skills has helped development of regional clusters. As India looks at a new wave of Make in India, we need to also consider the likely massive requirements of talent. Typically, global giants believe in scale. Some of the newer initiatives such as computers, batteries and semiconductors will also intrinsically require scale. Consistent competency development must be a simultaneous nation-wide effort. The newer Indian Institutes of Technology (IITs), Indian Institutes of Information Technology (IIITs) and the Indian Institutes of Management (IIMs) that have been so successfully set up in tier 2 cities and in the far-flung regions of the nation indicate that there could be a new wave of government-industry-academic collaboration.

Transform through Education

An effective Make in India initiative can happen not merely in India's industries or firms but more fundamentally through India's schools and colleges. The Indian educational system needs uniformity of high standards, encouragement of creativity, openness of evaluation and continuous bridging of theory and application. In the current India, quality is heavily tiered in terms of categories and brands of schools and colleges. While some differentiation across institutions is inevitable even in advanced nations (like between Ivy League and other institutions), the kinds of differentials that are allowed to perpetuate between different boards of education, different types of public and private educational institutions and institutes of national importance and several other tiers in India are huge, and in many cases discriminatory. A uniformly high quality of education on a pan-India basis has been elusive. The New Education Policy should address this gap effectively.

While this would take time, there is an urgent need for some quick reforms too. One way would be to dedicate the final semesters of each course to finishing courses which align the students to the industries of their choice rather than to desultory project assignments in which the randomly allotted firms and students have no shared interest. The finishing courses would comprise generic toolkit such as communication, collaboration, project management and networking skills, and specific industry toolkit such as machine learning and artificial intelligence in respect of information technology industry, quality assurance, and regulatory compliance in respect of pharmaceutical industry, mechatronics, and robotics in respect of machine tool industry, genetics, and epigenetics for biotechnology industry, and so on. The finishing courses should be nationally standardised and should be of such rigor that a student of any institution should be on par or above the best of global educational standards. Availability of such skill optimisation would make India a natural destination for Make in India realisation.

Together we succeed

It is important to realise that a nation cannot compete in the long term only on low wages or other cost arbitrage. China has, no doubt, become the world's workshop, in a manner of speaking, because of low wages and other manufacturing cost factors. However, as wages in China started rising, global MNCs have started looking at countries such as Vietnam and Bangladesh for locating their production bases. While different studies and agencies give different wage levels, it appears, from a formal manufacturing perspective, that Bangladesh is one of the lowest with a monthly average wage of around USD 300, with India being at around USD 700 and China at around 1100 while Taiwan, Singapore and South Korea being between USD 1000 and 5000. India's wage differential with China has not led to doubling of production bases in India or a major manufacturing migration from China – the lesson being that cost arbitrage could be a transitory advantage. India needs to offer a mix of national competencies and comparative advantages as discussed in this chapter to attract and retain global investments in the country.

While India has many industry associations, almost all of them have agendas related to policy reforms. Macroeconomic factors remain their paramount engagement. Skill upgradation is seen to be the task and responsibility, or even a unique competitive advantage, of each individual firm. Many firms are reluctant to open themselves to the pathways and success factors that determine competitiveness through intra-industry collaborative dialogue. Let us take the example of upgrading rail infrastructure to a level of bullet train network. This would require most modern track making and coach making technologies. If the existing railway wagon firms such as Integral Coach Factory, BEML, Kalindee Rail, Texmaco, Stone India, and Titagarh Wagons (and 12 others) do not upgrade their capabilities together there is little chance of Make in India being successful in this sector. Similar logic would apply to indigenous manufacture of new generation telecommunication gear, defence equipment or power plants.

Global Competitiveness

The national psychology must change from one of exulting over the relative superiority of firms against indigenous benchmarks to one of demanding absolute superiority of global standards. When there are reports of certain indigenous cars failing safety tests or certain products lagging packaging requirements, the concerned industries must collaborate to develop and validate product platforms and testing templates that meet global customer standards. Even granting that some of such global concerns tend to be subterfuge for non-tariff barriers, there is merit in industry-wide analysis of causes and development of solutions. Higher level of skills when pursued by individual firms may make individual firms competitive relative to other Indian firms but industry-wide actions make the entire industry competitive relative to global firms. This transformation would influence global industries to move into India as their preferred manufacturing destination. Consistency of competence across the industries as a national comparative advantage is the key to the success of Make in India revolution. Core competency for the future would lie in securing dominance in futuristic digital technologies.

Digital Futureproofing

The Centre's focus on futuristic digital technologies such as artificial intelligence, machine learning, robotics, IoT, blockchains, analytics and reskilling thereof, has been prominently articulated. This requires huge investments by the governments and private sector. The Union Budget 2023 has proposed an allocation of Rs 16,361 crore for Ministry of Science and Technology. Ideally, this should lead to a chain reaction with all the companies' committing funds for such digital technologies in their respective domains. India can find surprising but important uses for such technologies. A self-driving tractor, for example, can release the farmer to pursue other important chores. A sensor platform can help farmers optimise water drawal as well as water usage. A drone could excel in spraying fertilizers more precisely without any health hazard that is entailed when humans undertake such tasks. IT industry should take a lead role in artificial intelligence even as higher institutes of technology must assume an intellectual leadership and technology prototyping role.

Chapter 17

Market, Innovation, Technology, and Enterprise (MITE)

Corporate Longevity for Indian Enterprise

As India liberalises and globalises further and as global markets have their shares of competition and protectionism, Indian entities can no longer look towards regulatory, market, and other India-unique enablers to achieve longevity by default. Instead, companies should focus on strategic and structural factors that enable longevity in the entity form to the maximum extent, failing which at least the going businesses. To achieve that, however, principles must be developed differently for different companies in different types of businesses. Focusing on six of the growth industries in India, this chapter attempts to synthesise four critical factors that would determine corporate longevity in a model called MITE.

Some Perspectives

Wall Street Journal published an interesting article on January 7, 2012, by Spencer E Ante on corporate longevity. This was based on a study of more than six million firms by management professors Charles I. Stubbart and Michael B. Knight who concluded that, in fact, only a tiny fraction of the huge stock of companies in America reached the age of 40. "Despite their size, their vast financial and human resources, average large firms do not 'live' as long as ordinary Americans," the authors concluded. Ante makes the case that the classic strategies of product focus and manufacturing scale offer little insulation against corporate mortality if they are not accompanied by integration of emerging technologies and businesses. Ante argues that corporate longevity would seem to be at stake as organisations grow large and become bureaucratic. Reviewing the histories of several companies, Ante proposes that a willingness to forsake seemingly successful products with newer emergent technologies, diversifying into new technologies and businesses, and ensuring innovation through organic effort or niche mergers and acquisitions offer the right recipe for corporate longevity.

Even more sobering is the thought that with the increasing pace of technological change even 40 years could be a long period unless firms are innovative and agile. It appears that pioneers or innovators themselves could be at risk of technological change. Eastman Kodak is a striking example of a company that pioneered photography but failed to keep pace with technological transformations in core photography as well as in social networking through photos. In contrast, IBM is an equally striking example of a company that pioneered personal computers but decided to sell off the personal computer business yet succeeded to grow beyond 100 years by embracing emerging products and businesses. HP pursued scale in its core business of personal computers with the acquisition of Compaq but found that scale in hardware needed to be matched by skills in software and timeliness. Apple, in contrast, has been open to let its new innovative products cannibalise its established products. Even though the popular products were innovative at the time of their introduction, Apple's policy of successive product innovations enabled the company ride new waves of growth with new waves of product innovation.

Another aspect that has been discussed in the article relates to mergers and acquisitions as a tool to grow. The acquisition of YouTube and Android and later of Motorola's mobile phone business are powerful examples of companies acquiring new skills and capabilities to continue to grow. This strategy needs to be differentiated from certain other types of mergers, especially in the healthcare sector, which merely aimed at achieving scale, augmenting pipelines, or saving costs. Acquisitions by big companies that are prompted by a dire need for emerging technologies and businesses do mean that the start-up companies that have vibrant and innovative technologies have low longevity. However, the role of such start-ups in enhancing longevity of the major acquiring companies cannot be overemphasised.

The Indian Context

The Indian context has been dramatically different from what obtains in a free market economy in that easy exit, closure or liquidation of businesses and legal entities has never been an easy option. In fact, prior to economic liberalisation such options did not even exist. Added to that, the fact that almost all private entities in India are promoter-driven with a lot of emotional attachment and family succession makes economics of growth secondary to sentiments of survival. As a result, despite lack of product renewal or financial strength, Indian entities tend to stay on in a gamely fashion. As a corollary, despite the growth opportunities that ownership changes and mergers could bring about, Indian entities are highly reluctant to consider such options.

The economic liberalisation has, no doubt, brought in a shift in mindset that recognised the relevance of industrial and business restructuring to phase out non-sustainable activities and integrate developmental strengths externally. In a sharp shift, Indian companies began to exercise such growth and longevity options in the global arena. A few examples that illustrate this trend are Tata Steel (Corus), Tata Motors (JLR), Tata Tea (Tetley), Tata Chemicals (British Salt), Fortis Healthcare (Quality Healthcare), Bharti Airtel (Zain), Hindalco (Novelis), and others. Similarly, many global companies have aimed at collaborating with or acquiring Indian companies to support their longevity needs. However, similar activity between companies in India has been much less prominent. Figure 17.1 illustrates that India has still a long way to go in terms of global innovation rankings.

GII Rank	Economy	Score
1	Switzerland	67.6
2	Sweden	64.2
3	United States	63.5
4	United Kingdom	62.4
5	Singapore	61.5
6	Finland	61.2
7	Netherlands	60.4
8	Germany	58.8
9	Denmark	58.7
10	Republic of Korea	58.6
40	India	38.1

Figure 17.1: India in Global Innovation Ranking 2023

Longevity Drivers

In the Indian context, the drivers of longevity are still not economic. The entry barriers that characterise the Indian markets have ensured longevity in some cases despite repeated threats of new entry by other companies. Manufacture of commercial vehicles is a classic example of the country-specific requirement in India. The need for service and spare parts infrastructure in every nook and corner of the vast country has enabled the established truck and bus manufacturers, Ashok Leyland and Tata Motors, erect nearly unassailable entry barriers. In some other cases, regulatory policies have enabled longevity at the cost of economics. All sectors which limited or prohibited foreign investments such as media, aviation, benefitted from an insulation that by default also enabled longevity.

There have, however, been firms with customer and society facing characteristics, and with technological and operational robustness, that consistently grew, and in the process achieved longevity. Nirma, a small-scale maker of soaps and detergents (founded in 1969) which challenged MNC hegemony in soaps and detergents and became a multi-million dollar enterprise with multiple businesses (current turnover of over Rs 7,000 crore) is a classic example. Several foreign and Indian firms, on the other hand, also have seen unprecedented longevity in India by focusing on the expanding needs of a growing population. Hindustan Unilever is a striking example of this facet. This list includes firms like ITC, which completed 100 years in India by successfully transforming itself from a tobacco and cigarette making company to a diversified giant in consumer, industrial and hospitality domains. Examples of select sectors and firms reflecting longevity are instructive.

Longevity Examples

India offers several examples of growth sectors and individual firms with longevity. These industries and firms help us identify the critical factors that support corporate longevity.

Heavy Industrial Corporations

India has, even from the pre-independence days, focused on the development of heavy industries. These represent a very wide spectrum; from public sector "declined but supported by the government" entities such as Jessop, Garden Reach, and Air India to growing and cyclically profitable corporations such as BHEL and ONGC, and several others, including private sector construction giants such as L&T. The determinants of longevity for such companies also vary significantly, from restructuring of unprofitable businesses and companies to investments in new technologies and additional capacities for growth. The longevity of the companies is linked to growth in infrastructure and industry and subject to competition from other major emerging countries such as China. Given the massive infrastructure needs in India, heavy industry, including capital goods and construction, would be a growth industry and the challenge lies in the governments and companies securing finance for infrastructure and heavy industry, and developing technologies to stay competitive.

Consumer Corporations

Consumer oriented corporations, mostly as subsidiaries or franchised brands of multinational corporations, have been in existence from the pre-independence days but have faced sub-optimal growth due to pre-liberalisation (pre-1992) government policies that controlled entry licenses and production capacities. Despite this, several Indian companies such as Nirma and CavinKare could establish and grow themselves into multi-million corporations from humble beginnings. More recently, Patanjali has grown rapidly and aggressively (with no-holds-barred outsourcing and advertising) as a domestic Ayurveda major in the FMCG space. Today, a level playing field exists that allows Indian and MNC subsidiaries to benefit from the rapid growth of the Indian economy, and the middle class and affluent class social segments. Corporate longevity should not be a question mark for the consumer companies, but competitiveness would surely determine the differential rates of survival and growth of such enterprises.

Information Technology Corporations

The Indian software companies have been in the forefront of India's globalisation, especially from the 1990s. The vast Indian talent pool has enabled the Indian Information Technology (IT) companies successfully conceptualise a global delivery model based on a combination of offshore and onshore software services. The model further extended to IT enabled services (ITES) such as Business Process Outsourcing (BPO). The successes of the IT and ITES companies has prompted global giants such as IBM, Accenture, KPMG, Cap Gemini, KPMG, Ernst & Young and Deloitte to set up and expand IT, ITES and other related knowledge service bases in India, and thus protect and grow their global service businesses. This domain, again, is an interesting case of level playing field of competition among entities of diverse national and ownership patterns. Given the geo-political realities of retaining jobs in the Western and Emerging worlds Indian companies in these domains are now challenged to seek a different globalisation model to continue to grow. Equally challenging has been the inability of Indian corporations to stay as the first movers in newer fields such as Artificial Intelligence and Generative AI. IT industry would need to double up its efforts in this direction.

Pharmaceutical Corporations

Like the IT industry, the pharmaceutical industry has been a great intellectual asset, and a competitive industrial hub of India. India is the home to the largest number of generic bulk drug and formulations facilities approved by the US FDA, UK MHRA and other international regulatory agencies. The global generics industry is dominated by the Indian bulk drug and formulation products. While the growth of the industry has so far been excellent, and any shakiness caused by the harmonisation of intellectual property regime was overcome with the double-digit growth of the domestic pharmaceutical market, the prognosis from a corporate longevity point remains challenging. Firstly, the Indian pharmaceutical industry is highly fragmented with scores of large scale players, hundreds of medium scale players and thousands of small scale companies. Secondly, the space that the Indian industry operates in is the generics space which is not only a tail-end play but also has a declining pipeline of new off-patent generic products. Thirdly, the industry is yet to take up the issues of quality and regulatory compliance as a national competency. Equally challenging has been the inability of the select Indian pharmaceutical firms that took to drug discovery to come up with any new chemical or molecular entities that have gone through all the phases of clinical trials and international regulatory approvals for global commercialisation. Clearly, the Indian pharmaceutical industry needs to rediscover itself with a new paradigm. The achievement by Orchid Pharma of approvals from the US FDA and EU regulatory authorities for its novel betalactamese inhibitor has been an exception, and needs to be emulated by others.

Automobile Corporations

The Indian automobile industry is a fascinating example of a stupendous 'rags to riches' growth. From an annual output of around 49,000 passenger vehicles of extremely obsolete designs in FY1973 to an annual output of over 4,580,000 vehicles of contemporary designs in FY2023 (nearly 100-fold increase in just 50 years), the industry has achieved an amazing rate of growth. Equally impressive have been the growth stories in other types of automobiles (commercial vehicles from 42,000 to 962,000 and two-wheelers from 121,000 to 15,860,000). The growth has been equally amazing in terms of the variety and technology of vehicles, covering two-wheelers and four-wheelers as well as three-wheelers, tractors, and construction equipment. Lately, electric vehicles have also been added to the range. Amongst the various growth industries, however, the automobile industry has traditionally been the most import dependent. Yet, the saga of Tata Motors and Mahindra & Mahindra in multiple product lines, and that of Ashok Leyland in truck and bus segments illustrates that Indian technologies could also achieve global level innovation and competitiveness. In particular, the design and manufacture of Nano small car, SUVs, and electric cars as well as turnaround of Jaguar-Land Rover by Tata Motors, and development of heavy trucks and electric buses by Ashok Leyland are indicative of the indigenous competitive capability and the growth potential for Indian automobile firms. The challenge, however, lies in the ability to innovate in premium segments and in designing cars that suit Indian road and driving conditions. The limited road infrastructure that could constrain the growth of the Indian automobile industry is also another challenge in the context of its low export competitiveness.

Electronics Corporations

If the Indian IT, automobile, and pharmaceutical sectors have been the high points of growth, the electronics industry has been a relative laggard. India's deficiency in electronics development and manufacture is in stark contrast to the global dominance that China and Taiwan as well as South Korea (in a more pioneering fashion) have achieved in the domain. That said, the recent progress of India in the manufacture of mobile phones, tablet computers, television sets and certain other electronics gear is reflective of the capability of the Indian electronics industry to develop new competencies and grow. Like automobile industry, the Indian electronics industry needs strong market-linked collaborative strengths to attract new product and manufacturing opportunities to the country. Accuracy of manufacture, finish of the products and low manufacturing cost seem to be the primary factors for the success of the electronics industry in China, independent of the availability of local market. Apple products constitute a good example of the global conquest through Chinese manufacture. It is notable that Apple has taken up assembly of Apple iPhones from India in a big way, and Tata Group has entered this indigenous Apple manufacturing ecosystem in an ambitious way. More than anything else, electronics industry demonstrates how competition and collaboration coexist on a global scale in contemporary industrial development. It is heartening that the Government of India has taken up manufacture of semiconductors as a priority.

Competition and Collaboration

Professor Michael Porter considers his Five Forces Theory, first propounded in his landmark book *Competitive Strategy: Techniques for Analyzing Industries and Competitors* as a common template that overrides industry differences through certain basic criteria. The five forces, namely competitive rivalry, bargaining power of customers, bargaining power of suppliers, threat of new entrants and threat of substitute products are applicable for all industries. According to Porter, the origin of profitability is identical irrespective of industry. Industry structure is a key determinant while whether the forces are benign or intense defines the level of profitability. In the 1990s, Yale School of Management professors Adam Brandenbuger and Bare Nalebuff in their book *Co-opetition* proposed the idea of a sixth force, "complementors" using the tools of game theory. In their model, complementors sell products and services that are best used in conjunction with a product or service from a competitor. Intel, which manufactures chips, and Apple which manufactures computers are considered complementors in this model. There could be, of course, situations, when both the complementors become competitors due to their integration and diversification strategies. Formulators of economic policy must understand how their economic policies impact the levels of competition and collaboration, across firms and industries.

MITE as a Longevity Model

The above discussion of the six growth industries of India helps formulation of a corporate longevity model. For the Indian enterprises, the key to longevity lies in understanding the importance of the four key factors of market, innovation, technology, and enterprise (or, entrepreneurship). Firstly, India itself offers a huge market, but the enterprises must be savvy enough to identify the markets and develop them aggressively with appropriate products and services. In addition, the international markets are available for the Indian companies to be won based on competitiveness. All the six industries discussed above teach us that markets are eager to be served by Indian companies. Secondly, the concept of level playing field has come to stay. Companies need to compete on factor advantages rather than on policy advantages. Yet, access to global factor advantages is also becoming possible to all global corporations. This implies that only those firms that are consistently innovative can be more competitive and enjoy the benefits of longevity. Start-up innovation provides the toehold, but continuous innovation alone can provide sustained growth. Thirdly, technology would be the core of competitive advantage. Those companies which deploy technology on an end-to-end basis, across the total value chain, would be more competitive than firms which deploy technology only in some areas, be it manufacturing or R&D. Fourthly, every company should remember its basic enterprising spirit and its entrepreneurial roots. Firms, as they become large, must preserve, and foster entrepreneurial spirit as an organisational DNA. As the WSJ article observes, the board rooms of high growth and high longevity corporations tend to be as entrepreneurial as those of successful start-up companies.

On a holistic basis, all the four factors are equally important but entrepreneurial spirit provides the fundamental corporate genetic drive to stay hungry and keep growing. As the companies become larger nationally and internationally, growth is often accompanied by bureaucracy, with multi-layering and multi-reporting. Firms fail to customise themselves to diverse markets and their needs, and instead attempt to find solutions in globally standardised products and services as well as business processes. The experience of the six growth industries suggests that an ability to customise and innovate across markets has helped certain Indian industries such as information technology and pharmaceuticals to take part in global growth while certain globalised industries such as automobile industry could achieve tremendous success in India by customising their products to local conditions. The strategies of even luxury car makers such as Range Rover, BMW, and Audi to offer their sedan and crossover vehicles respectively in India indicates the recognition of the need for local customisation, covering both urban and rural markets. Indian enterprises committed to global longevity must first internationalise their organisations to understand the markets, innovate on their products for customisation and build the technological base in the value chain to manage product variety with productivity. The MITE model of corporate longevity provides the might to Indian enterprises to seek and achieve perpetual growth. An important backbone of the strategy would be to develop more innovation clusters in India that compare with the best in the world. Figure 17.2 illustrates the Indian strengths and weaknesses in innovation.

Rankings for India (2020–2023)			
GII Year	**GII**	**Innovation inputs**	**Innovation outputs**
2020	48	57	45
2021	46	57	45
2022	40	42	39
2023	40	46	35

Strengths		**Weaknesses**	
Rank	**Indicator name**	**Rank**	**Indicator name**
1	Domestic market scale, bn PPP$	131	Environmental performance
5	ICT services exports, % total trade	110	Tertiary inbound mobility, %
6	VC received, value, % GDP	106	Females employed w/ advanced degrees, %
8	Intangible asset intensity, top 15, %	103	ICT use
9	Finance for startups and scaleups	101	ICT access
9	Unicorn valuation, % GDP	101	Pupil-teacher ratio, secondary
10	Domestic industry diversification	99	Knowledge-intensive employment, %
11	Graduates in science and engineering, %	86	School life expectancy, years
13	Global corporate R&D investors, top 3, mn US$	81	Researchers, FTE/mn pop.
16	Gross capital formation, % GDP	55	Entertainment and media market/th pop. 15-69

Figure 17.2: Indian Strengths and Weaknesses in Innovation

Science and Technology

Economic Survey 2022-23 observed that science, technology, and innovation offer instrumental and intrinsic value for society. It states that as India emerges as one of the world's largest economies, it needs to gradually move from being a net consumer of knowledge to becoming a net producer. India's R&D investment at USD 65.2 billion is just 10 percent of that of USA and 13 percent of China's (on PPP basis). India has 255 researchers per million of population versus 1,585 of China and 4,452 of USA. The Survey brings out the point that India was spending more on R&D as percentage of GDP than countries like China when China was at the same level of GDP per capita. However, such countries began committing huge increases to R&D with increased prosperity while India began lagging. Private investments in research lagged public investments which only amplified the knowledge gap further. Of the top 2,500 R&D global spenders, there are 301 Chinese companies and just 26 Indian companies. Of these 26, 19 are in just three sectors: pharmaceuticals, automobiles, and software. India has no firms in the top ten R&D sectors as opposed to China that has presence in each of them.

Chapter 18

The New World Order

Strategies for Managers

The orderly management of global affairs requires at the core a stable and growth-oriented economic environment. Within this, it is given that firms and nations compete. The underlying theme must, however, be the overall good of humanity. Science, technology, management, and entrepreneurship are critical elements of this process. The principal purpose of management is to establish and grow businesses profitably. Managers are engaged in planning and execution of various activities towards the fulfilment of this purpose. In this process, managers are required to define and understand the business in the context of the environmental opportunities and challenges.

The recession of 2008 and 2009, consequent to the global financial meltdown taught the governments and central bankers many lessons. As a result, although Covid-19 pandemic hit the globe in 2020 with near disastrous economic impact, the nations could quickly recover. Science, technology, management, and entrepreneurship played their part in this, be it through the development of effective vaccines at an unprecedented speed (one year as against ten years) or stimulation of economic activity (through injection of massive global liquidity).

New World Order

A new world order is now developing with Global South playing an increasingly important role. While China had established itself as the second largest global economy, after the US, India is now racing to become a USD 6 trillion-dollar economy, and the world's third largest by 2028. Global governments, firms and investors are convinced that India is the brightest spot in the global economic canvas. And to that, we would need to add the rich cultural heritage that India has. Indian business must define itself as one of the important harbingers of the socio-economic transformation. Firms must increasingly focus on serving global markets as opposed to only domestic markets. Extending further, firms are not content with mere exports but are more intent on being a part of global network through Make in India. Firms, therefore, need to understand the new world order that could determine their effectiveness.

The phrase "new world order" does not lend itself to easy definition. As vision expands and as competition intensifies, a business cannot be defined in terms of only product configuration or market opportunity. Several economic, industrial, social, and cultural factors impact the businesses of industries and firms. A dynamic world order also provides its own share of changing opportunities and challenges. Multinational firms seeking India's consumption market must participate in India's socioeconomic development through Make in India. Both Indian and overseas enterprises must embark on new unchartered paths of science, technology, products, and services. A multipolar world must consider that India is poised to play a much larger role. Figure 18.1 outlines the characteristics of multipolar world.

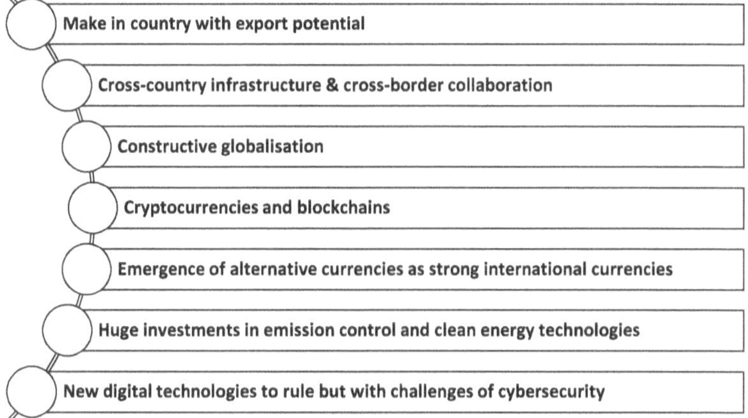

Figure 18.1: The Characteristics of Multipolar World

The new world order needs to be viewed in terms of the following: (i) economic environment, (ii) industrial competitiveness (iii) social imperatives, and (iv) cultural factors. Each of these brings forth certain challenges to managers and leaders.

(i) Economic Environment

Events, from time to time, bring out how economic conditions can turn volatile, unsettling nations and industries in the process. The economic environment is characterised by four aspects: (i) highly uncertain global liquidity conditions (ii) volatile and unpredictable exchange rates (iii) investments in infrastructure as economic stimulus, and (iv) geo-political developments altering economic opportunities and enhancing challenges. Economic forecasting, never a precise science, is now required to be much more robust and truly multi-factorial. Icebergs of asset bubbles move under apparently placid economic waters. The unpredictability of economic environment renders any planning for economic development or recovery hazardous.

Alternatively, global liquidity can be considered the sixth competitive force that adds an entirely new dimension to Porter's theory of competitive strategy (see my book, "Competitive

Strategy: A Contemporary Retake" for a comprehensive discussion of the competitive power of the economic forces). The political framework has also been evolving over the last few years leading to new economic opportunities and challenges. Governments in advanced economies are turning more protectionist, introducing invisible barriers in the path of globalisation whereas governments in emerging economies, especially China and India, are pursuing aggressive growth to move up the global economic order. Companies are required to have vastly different skill sets including their own national comparators and risk mitigating strategies to provide a safe path for their global operations.

(ii) *Industrial Competitiveness*

The emerging industrial framework is characterised by four new dimensions: (i) an accelerated level of technological convergence in product functionalities, (ii) an unprecedented level of competitive frenzy among firms, (iii) a twin and simultaneous pursuit of differentiation and cost-competitiveness, (iv) a near universal requirement for high-end technologies, and (iv) a continuously upskilling talent base. High-end technologies include advanced electronics such as semiconductors, sensors, digital technologies such as artificial intelligence, and genetic and biotechnologies that redefine life and living, all of these backed by genuine talent that can take industries on a new creativity path.

Industrial competitiveness requires continuous investments in R&D and manufacture, better remuneration for intellectual talent and a quest for profitability in highly competed markets, which are characterised by increasingly shorter product lifecycles. Management of firms is a challenge whether pertaining to sunrise sectors or mature sectors. Industrial competitiveness is determined by patenting capability on one hand and manufacturing efficiency on the other. So far, innovation has been an advanced market play while efficiency has been an emerging market option. Emerging economies now have a greater scope in redefining the balance in their favour, with increased share of innovation and dominant share of manufacturing, provided the opportunity is seized in the right manner.

(iii) *Social Needs*

The social framework offers certain positive and encouraging triggers for a new world order: (i) societies across the world are increasingly conscious of the perils of profligate economies, (ii) people are more aware now than at any time in the past on environmental protection, global warming, and renewable energy, (iii) the governments and the societies are seized of the need to focus on quality education at a universal level to achieve national level competitiveness through human resource base. Firms can do their bit in social transformation through their Environmental, Social and Governance (ESG) approaches, and Diversity, Equity, and Inclusion (DEI).

Globally as a whole, societies today are better informed and more demanding in terms of quality-of-life enablers such as housing, healthcare, education, transportation, clean environment, and food security. America has, though belatedly, recognised the chinks in its social armour, for example, on healthcare. Japan and Korea are endeavouring to retain their competitiveness based on the traditional competitive nature of their society. China has viewed its massive drive for aggressive growth as a means for social uplift but is realizing that growth that is powered by asset bubbles may not be sustainable at high levels. India is endeavouring with new paradigms to realise its potential with a strong growth thrust, maintaining the delicate rural-urban balance.

(iv) *Cultural Factors*

The cultural framework is a less studied aspect of globalisation and the new world order. Globalisation and growth typically require integration of cross-cultural resources as well as catering to their specific needs. Despite the Internet and information revolution, countries and societies remain rooted in their respective cultural systems. For example, without being judgemental, one may hypothesise from a business and economic perspective that American culture continues to be transactional and impersonal, Japanese culture insular and cocooned, Korean culture aggressive and expansionist, Chinese culture competitive and domineering, and Indian culture philosophical and emotional.

The expectations of local work force and local customers and the intentions of global multinational corporations are often at variance. Lack of understanding on issues of science and technology, biodiversity, and social relevance often impedes industrial development. The issue of genetically modified crops is just one example, where objective science rather than commerce should have influenced the debate and outcomes. But there could be issues in which culture could trump both science and commerce. It is important for global MNCs and Indian companies to frame their global aspirations and execution, integrating the cultural anchors of their markets in deep consideration.

Strategies for Managers

Managers, and educational institutions committed to management development, have a lot to unlearn and learn, to be effective in the new world order. Management programmes must be contextual and dynamic, in tune with the global trends. They also need to be sharper and contemporary in terms of conceptual and analytical tools. Traditional theories and practices of management must be potentially supplemented, and in some cases, revised with more relevant perspectives. Managers must develop combinations of skill sets that can help them confidently tackle the varied challenges in the economic, industrial, social and cultural frameworks mentioned earlier.

Reskilling Managers and Leaders

India cannot remain only a cost arbitrage country. With rapid technological changes driving fundamental structural changes in industry, there is a great need for India to develop and offer more innovative products and services. The challenges and opportunities faced by the Indian information technology industry with the advent of artificial intelligence, machine learning and deep learning are indicative of the need for proactively reskilling the workforce. For this to happen the managers and leaders need to reequip themselves more proactively. Conventional leadership and management development programmes would not be sufficient. One valuable way for managers and leaders would be to evaluate how they can contribute to fundamental transformations in the economy. For example, leaders and managers in agrochemical industry must be seized of moving from chemical-based fertilizers and insecticides into bio-pesticides. Those in automobile and battery industries must collaborate on how they can make the automobile industry completely electric. Educational institutions and information technology companies should position India as a global leader in online education. Reskilling at managerial and leadership levels must comprise identifying and executing on mega-trends that lead to socio-economic transformation. Figure 18.2 illustrates the key managerial skills for a globalized world.

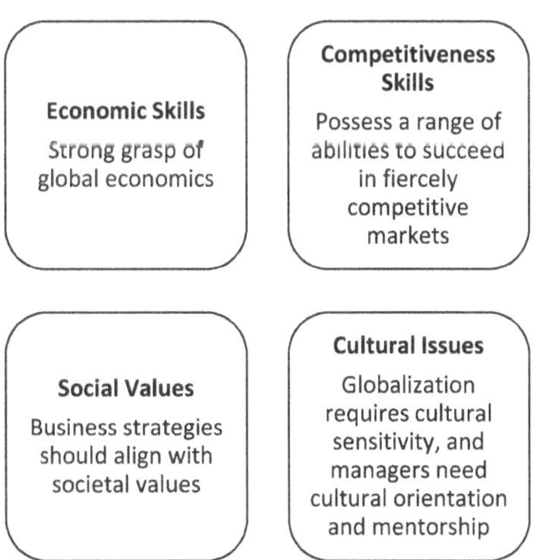

Figure 18.2: Key Managerial Skills for a Globalized World

(i) Economic Skills

Contemporary managers must possess a deeper understanding of national and international economies and the inter-linkages between economic and industrial development on one hand and social and community development on the other. Economic forecasting, never an exact science despite the proliferation of statistical tools, needs to be taken up as a key methodology for understanding future economic trends and opportunities, as well as risks. Making firms self-reliant in terms of capital structure and accessing international funding options in a timely manner are two critical tasks for managers. Financial prudence and reliance on savings rather than borrowings need to be the hallmarks of a good financial manager. Exercise of caution and display of capability while resorting to exotic financial products will help the managers serve their companies well.

An understanding of international tax laws and international forex trading would be an important addition to the customary tool kit of a typical manager. In several cases, manufacturing and supply chain logic is often distorted by tax and exchange considerations. As India's managers aim to be a part of global manufacturing and supply chain network, knowledge of these economic aspects help them negotiate with their MNC counterparts the logic of global investment, sourcing and supply decisions.

Globalisation has led to an increased shift of resources to emerging countries. This runs contrary to the aspiration of human talent in emerging markets to seek employment in advanced nations. Global outsourcing tends to reduce the need for external talent in advanced countries. Managers of education systems and human resource systems must reframe their talent development strategies to focus on advanced capabilities to position Indian talent as being internationally competitive. Management education programmes, or for that matter scientific and technical education programmes, must focus on building advanced scientific and technical skills to prepare professionals for careers in advanced domains (not necessarily in advanced countries, of course).

(ii) Competitiveness Skills

Industrial or business managers must be well-versed in competitiveness skills, to meet the intensely fierce market conditions. Multiple abilities, capabilities and skill sets are required to manage industrial competitiveness; for example, an ability to reduce time to market, an ability to balance continuous investments with sustained profitability, an ability to manage global operations and logistics, and skills in global procurement and supply chain optimisation are some of the essentials for the new manager.

Equally important would be the ability to achieve greater design and manufacturing variety without compromising scheduling simplicity and inventory optimisation. An understanding of industry structure and competitive forces is essential for the managers. The requirement to achieve product differentiation with low-cost manufacture and an ability to serve larger markets even with niche products pose new strategic and operational challenges for managers.

Competitiveness is a function of scale and scope as well. As firms seek to acquire higher scale and scope, through organic or inorganic growth, managers must also learn to balance business aggression with financial prudence. They must also balance growth-driving leverage with stability-providing internal generations. The recession of the last two years teaches us that companies which are aggressive but prudentially managed have not only successfully withered the impact of recession but are also well poised to grow in the recovery phase.

(iii) Social Values

The products and services that are identified through business analysis and business execution need to reflect normative social values. Increased purchasing power no doubt vests in the society a certain degree of consumerism and profligacy. It is incumbent on the part of business managers to focus on product and manufacturing strategies that are good for the society. Energy saving equipment, green buildings, fuel-efficient vehicles, cloud computing and storage, web-based services, digital publishing, renewable energy, and alternate fuels represent some areas where managerial passion for environment and society could help corporations become better citizens.

Equally important would be the need to develop healthcare solutions for poorer sections of the society so that affordable medicines are available. In countries like India, where agriculture plays an important role in the national economy, the rural sector needs to be preserved by bringing modern amenities with appropriate adaptation to rural consumers. ITC's e-choupal, for example, is a great example of how corporate vision and IT management can leverage modern technology for rural commercialisation. Dr C K Prahalad has propounded, with several case examples, how unique business and technological models can help companies find fortune at the bottom of the pyramid.

(iv) Cultural Issues

Globalisation requires managers to interact with multiple nationalities and multiple cultures. Many corporations undertake cultural orientation programmes to enable their executives and managers deal with cultural ramifications with sensitivity. No such programme, however, is perfect. In some cases, they tend to be mere facades, turning out to be counter-productive in the end. Leaders and managers who have worked in overseas environments can act as mentors for executives moving over to other countries. Indian managerial education needs to integrate cultural training into managerial processes through such mentorship programmes.

Management education has a different cultural implication as well. In India, management education is seen to lead persons into general management as a distinct profession. The reality, however, is that management education provides certain conceptual and analytical tools relevant for any professional or specialist to grasp and solve real-life business, scientific or technological issues better. As a matter of fact, Japan, the world leader in industrial operations, has very few MBAs. In USA, it is not uncommon for scientists and technologists to acquire management education simply to hone their skills. With management education, specialists are enabled to conduct domain management more efficiently and more productively in a holistic organisational and business setting. Management education must be seen more as a value-add to all the functions and domains rather than as an enabler for a stand-alone managerial career.

Summary

The fortunes of a business are intertwined with the evolution of the world order. Economic environment, industrial competitiveness, societal expectations, and cultural moorings dictate the opportunities and challenges of the world order. Managers need to retool their strategies to navigate through global liquidity concerns, achieve industrial competitiveness with innovation and efficiency, adapt their strategies to societal needs and integrate with diverse cultures to understand needs and deliver solutions. The more adept managers are in their domains and at their tasks, the more prosperous would be the businesses and industries, positively impacting the national economy. Economic Survey 2017-18 came- up with the formulation of a Twin Balance Sheet problem in India. Holistic managerial skills are required for the nation to have one strong, singular balance sheet.

TBS – Twin Balance Sheet Problem

Economic Survey 2017-18 came up with the nomenclature of Twin Balance Sheet or TBS. There are two issues which are left unaddressed though. The Survey brought out that gross

NPA ratio of scheduled commercial banks increased from 9.6 percent in March 2017 and to 10.2 percent in September 2017. The stressed advances ratio rose from 12.1 percent to 12.2 percent. The situation with reference to public sector banks (PSBs) was worse. GNPA ratio of PSBs increased from 12.5 percent to 13.5 percent in March and September 2017. Stressed advances ratio of PSBs increased to 15.6 and 16.2 percent in the same periods. As against this, the Survey admits that bank recapitalisation caters to only 1.3 percent of gross advances. The situation began changing over the last few years after the Government of India brought in the Insolvency and Bankruptcy Code of India to clean up the NPA situation. That said, the data on recoveries by financial institutions (euphemistically called haircuts) indicates recoveries of dues being as low as 30 percent. Clearly, the scars of NPAs on the banking system would get ameliorated with time as the progress achieved through Insolvency and Bankruptcy Code is maintained. There must be complete clarity on how the banking system would systemically prevent a recurrence of the NPA problem. That's why the propositions in this book that seek to ensure solvency rather than scurry around for insolvency are relevant.

The June 2023 Financial Stability Report (FSR) by RBI highlights the robustness of India's banking sector, showcasing improvements in key indicators such as return on assets, reduced non-performing assets, and increased provision coverage. The report emphasizes the resilience of banks under stress scenarios and introduces the Banking Stability Indicator (BSI) for a comprehensive assessment. Learning from the Twin Balance Sheet (TBS) syndrome, the report underscores the need for prudent risk governance and collaboration between banks and the corporate sector to ensure sustained economic growth.

Chapter 19

Rebalancing Leadership, Management, and Administration

Some Philosophical Conundrums

Leadership is the process of setting a vision, crafting a strategy, and ensuring execution for an organisation. Management (including administration) is the process of doing things (including getting things done). Without management and administration, orderly and directed development of organisations and societies would be difficult. Over the last several decades, however, leadership has been positioned as a unique responsibility of leaders at the top and management has become more identified with regular organisational and business development, while administration has become identified with ongoing economic and social development. Leadership is seen as a vision- and strategy-inspired instrument of transformation. Management is seen as a process and metrics driven instrument of competitiveness while administration is seen as a compliance- and welfare-driven instrument of governance. On the flip side, leadership, with little accountability, could be reckless in its deployment of resources for future, and management, with excessive accountability, could be micro-controlling in its quest for efficiency. Administration in its search of a formula to achieve both growth and equity could vacillate between the two imperatives, which need to be harmonized. Figure 19.1 compares leadership and management.

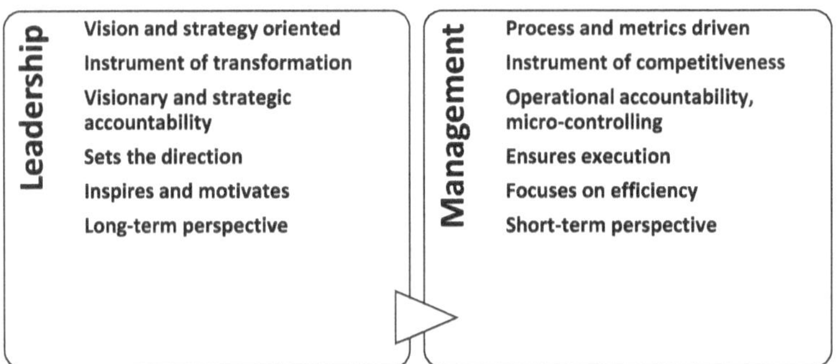

Figure 19.1: Leadership and Management

As my book "Leadership for India, Inc.: An Experiential Treatise" discusses at length, leadership, management, and administration are required as a composite whole. The attempts by different practitioners and theoreticians, proposing a greater separation between leadership and management on one hand, and management and administration on the other serve only limited purposes. When leadership, management and administration are synchronised for planning and execution, integration happens. For example, technical domains may be different from leadership, management, and administration but all the three are interrelated in planning and execution. Technical operations similarly are intertwined with technology foresight, technology planning, technology management, and so on. Technology drives R&D on one hand and manufacturing on the other. Segmented thought processes which try to maximise parts miss out that the whole is being sub-optimised in such segmented processes. With challenges of federal structures in administration and global structures in management and leadership, there is a need to recapture the fundamental purpose of leadership, management, and administration. The key purpose of all leadership, management and administration needs to be development (not necessarily growth) with equity (not necessarily with equality). This chapter falls back on one of the most fundamental branches of study, namely philosophy, to restore the perspectives.

Philosophy

Philosophy is the study of fundamental aspects of knowledge and practice, abstraction and reality, and perception and existence. The objective of philosophy as a branch of study is to vest one with wisdom. As illustrated In Figure 19.2, enquiry, and logic as well as hypothesis and validation form the bedrocks of the study of philosophy in any field. While the Western philosophical thought owes much to Plato, Aristotle and Socrates, many others added to subsequent philosophical streams. In contrast, Hindu, Buddhist, Jain, and other oriental philosophical streams had a hoary past. The Hindu Vedic Upanishads are the earliest exponents of philosophy in the world. Indian philosophy, in general, brings significant analytical rigour to metaphysical issues and enquires about the existential reality through the nature and function of human psyche. The ultimate purpose of Hindu philosophy is the attainment of 'moksha' or 'nirvana' (salvation).

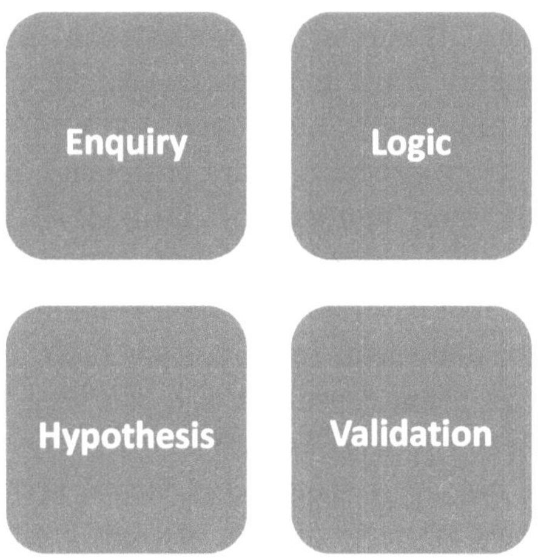

Figure 19.2: Bedrocks of the Study of Philosophy

Modern philosophy builds on the fundamentals of ancient philosophical wisdom with a contemporary tweak. Indian leaders and philosophers, Sarvepalli Radhakrishnan, Sri Aurobindo,

Mahatma Gandhi, Madan Mohan Malaviya, Bala Gangadhar Tilak, Rabindranath Tagore, B R Ambedkar, and Jiddu Krishnamurti, to name a few, sought to superimpose contemporary social imperatives on fundamental philosophical premises to generate new developmental ethos. It is a matter of regret that business and economics have not had philosophers who brought to bear such contemporary tweaks in organisational systems. These disciplines have produced leaders driven for execution or academicians focussed on strategizing. Only Mahatma Gandhi brought in valuable social and economic philosophical underpinnings to business. The world would be a better place if professionals dedicated to management and administration begin to apply principles of philosophy to what these disciplines aim to achieve.

Logic

'Tarka Shastra' is a Sanskrit term for the domain related to the philosophy of dialectics, logic, and reasoning. Logic is the foundation of philosophy. The logic for business, or 'business logic' as is commonly phrased, is pursued by professionals. Some interpret it as improving quality of life and some as providing more value for money. Almost universally, businesses desire to be in perpetual growth mode - more products, more customers, more revenues, more profits, and more market capitalisation! All things that are synthetic, that is all manmade goods, come from natural resources. Everyone knows that natural resources are not unlimited. Today's oil, gas, mineral and metal resources are built up over several centuries but are being consumed at a rate that would exhaust them over just a few decades. Logic, therefore, says that industrial progress as we see today (newer and varied products in larger quantities) is going to stutter and stop one day. While the principles of conservation are invoked time to time, the fundamental drive to convert natural resources to synthetic products has not stopped.

The only living activity that is self-sufficient is organic agriculture that is rooted in the soil, nourished by rains, and nurtured by seasons. Even if all the modern-day products (from tractors to fertilizers, and from processing to packaging) disappear, agriculture would remain as the sole economic activity that would help humans survive. Management and administration are not adequately recognising the primal role of agriculture in human life and are not doing enough to ensure a virtuous agricultural ecosystem. Logically, there should be more institutes of rural management and there should be more aspirants for diplomas in agricultural management offered by the IIMs. Unfortunately, the contrary seems to be true. Logically again, 'ruralisation' should have greater priority over urbanisation, and agriculture must continue to be the dominant national culture. Logic also suggests that economic responsibility at local community level leads to broader economic strength at national level.

Local Economic Leadership

OECD in its publication titled *Local Economic Leadership, 2015* discusses the importance of local economic leadership in developing micro-regions. While democratic governance in India goes far beyond that in any other jurisdiction other government in terms of grassroots administration at village level thanks to the legacy left behind by Mahatma Gandhi, there is still a lot that can be done. Instructively, the OECD paper urges business leadership to contribute to local economic leadership by undertaking the following activities: advocacy of local causes with stakeholders including governments, promotion of local economy, encouragement of regional collaboration, building of consensus, sponsorship of specific activities, providing their knowhow for local development, communication of local needs and accomplishments, providing of organisational vehicles, internationalisation, and so on. The Report quotes the example of Hamburg's 350-year-old Chamber of Commerce in promoting local economic development. India has a significant history of local development. By looping in businesses, and where necessary international organisations like OECD, India can provide impetus to this critical activity of local self-administration and local economic development.

Rationality

Equally unfortunately, however, not all logic can be followed, especially when one must contend with a legacy of what fruits of development, as commonly understood, bring to population. With economic development, what has not been necessary becomes commonplace, and what has been an option becomes fundamentally necessary. Economic development surprises and intoxicates people with surprisingly newer and richer products. A television three decades ago cost no more than Rs 10,000 but today advertisements galore for televisions that cost more than Rs 300,000. Development is modern day economic marijuana; like the cannabis has its medical uses, development has its economic uses, but the primary risk of intoxication and addiction will never cease. However logical it may be from a philosophical angle to moderate profligacy that masquerades as development, the appeal of development can neither be wished away nor rebelled against.

Rationality offers a solution when logic is stymied by legacy. Rationality requires conserving as much as consuming. As a seemingly bizarre but rational example, rationality may require that all mineral water and soft beverage plants must be located only at river mouths which see loss of millions of cusecs of water every day, especially in rainy seasons. The mineral water park must have its own aqua reservoir filled with water which would have otherwise gone waste to the sea. Another way to look at conservation could be that soft beverages must be made only with desalinated water; if people have an aversion to drink desalinated beverages, so be it - as the result would only be conservation of water. Another example of rationality could be that any large-scale electronics firm should set up its own electronic waste recycling facility along with the main plant. Another mandate could be that there will no longer be any naturally aspirated engine but only turbocharged intercooled engine, as another example (until of course electric or hydrogen power-packs become commercially available on a large scale!).

Hypothesis

One bedrock of philosophy is hypothesis. Without hypothesis there can be no discussion, without discussion there can be no debate, without debate there can be no inclusivity, and without inclusivity there can be no progress. It is important that leaders, managers, and administrators proceed based on intelligent hypotheses. While there is a strong element of intuition in successful management and leadership as well as in administration, intuition does not occur always; it kicks in somewhat spontaneously and selectively. In addition, intuition also works on hypothesis. Philosophy as a branch of study focuses as much on gaining knowledge through prior art as on building knowledge through forward looking hypothesis.

Managers and administrators feel that they are rational if they are planners. Planning, however, is not hypothesising. Development of hypotheses is a more subtle form of thinking about and feeling for other persons (stakeholders, for example) and other events (competition, for example). Every route that is taken up as part of a planning process must have a solid hypothesis. If the government believes that fiscal incentives are necessary to innovate in India, there must be an underlying hypothesis on investor behaviour and expectations (and not on GDP growth rate, *per se*). Hypothesis is not the equivalent of assumption; the latter being another superficial component of the planning process. A view on 'action-reaction' (quantitative easing leading to reversal of recession, for example) is not hypothesis either. In this case, the hypothesis is probably one of restoring people's faith in an economic future.

Validation

The fourth pillar of philosophy is validation. Science is built on experimental validation. Management and administration have a lower scope for validation because they deal with people and require rather irreversible commitments. Validation usually occurs in managerial and administrative spheres by past results or by pilot projects for future. If hypothesis construction is perceptively carried out based on past results, validation has a lesser role to play. However, when major initiatives are undertaken validation of hypothesis through pilot projects is well merited. Validation is fundamental in all technical areas and equipment as well as process related aspects but is a challenge when people and culture related aspects are involved. Progressive validation is a useful way to ensure execution perfection and improve the quality of hypothesis itself.

When definite public good is involved through breakthrough concepts, it makes sense to ensure maximum coverage in a risk-proof manner. A highly fuel-efficient car deserves a universal hypothesis with little validation. A solar powered car may require progressive development of concept through progressive validation. Philosophical approach to business and administration requires that resources are conserved by not throwing them into arena without validation. Whether a Singapore type of capital is viable in Andhra Pradesh may have answers in how the Gachi Bowli development in Hyderabad has taken wings. The hypothesis that development skyrockets land prices, and escalating land prices benefit owners is a hypothesis, for example, that can be validated with the examples of New Raipur and such other developmental regions.

Wisdom

The life of a philosopher is lonely and controversial. In a world that seeks speed, a philosopher's approach of logic, rationality, hypothesis, and validation could be seen as time consuming. A philosopher has, many a time, few followers, and many critics. Even a saint-philosopher as great as Sri Ramanuja had to face opposition. Leadership has an important role in furthering positive philosophical perspectives for management and administration. Management and administration which seek conformity of thought are not the natural habitats for philosophy. Yet, these are the very domains which could benefit from application of philosophical principles. Corporations and public bodies which have departments and officers for compliance must also institutionalise cells and sentinels for philosophical enquiry and objectivity. A judicious amalgamation of philosophy in an organisational ecosystem leads to balanced economic and social development, rooted in wisdom. In today's economic context, a business philosopher must speak his mind to guide the future course on appropriate premises.

Recapitalisation Focus

Dr Y V Reddy, former RBI Governor in his K L N Prasad Memorial Lecture at Hyderabad on February 01, 2018, brought forth several challenges facing the Government in strengthening the banking system. While doing so, he pointed out that the Government by redirecting a larger share of the first tranche of recapitalisation to weaker banks has gone against the recommendations of the Fourteenth Finance Commission which recommended that recapitalisation should be directed towards select and better performing banks, asking the weaker and non-performing banks to manage their asset portfolio within the available capital. This by itself was a tall order when some of the best-known banks like State Bank of India and Bank of Baroda posted losses due to NPA provisioning and mark-to-market losses on bonds. Dr Reddy also said that unlike the environment of the 1969 when major banks were nationalised, the context of banking in India had since transformed with a mix of public and private sector banks. Within the public sector, there came to be a mix of public and private ownership. Foreign investors started assuming a presence in both public sector and private sector banks. Going forward from the 2020s, apart from what Dr Reddy stated, the operational world of banking is likely to be disrupted by cryptocurrencies, blockchains and various other digital trends. Indian Government needs to be specially focussed on the efficiency, strength, and resilience of the Indian banking system to be able to serve the nation well. The Government of India, over the last seven years, has done well to clean up the non-performing assets of the banks through the Insolvency and Bankruptcy Code of India. This, again, demonstrates great administrative leadership that restored strength and resilience in the Indian banking sector while reviving the industrial assets onto a growth path instead of allowing them to get liquidated.

Chapter 20

The Seeds that Become Trees

A New Logic for India's Industrial Forestry

There are many sayings that demonstrate the power of small seeds that could grow into massive trees. After all, nature is all about free fall of seeds in fertile lands turning into bountiful forests, duly aided by rain and shine. In a nation's life too, industrial, and economic growth tends to be based on seeds of innovation and manufacture. A few governmental moves (eg., heavy engineering thrust of the yesteryears or the semiconductor passion of today), or a few individual initiatives (eg., Jamsetji Tata's steel vision, despite the colonial past or Sunil Mittal's telecom passion, despite the massive investments) turned out or would turn out to be major transformational revolutions years later. The drivers of development are simple and straightforward in many cases; however, only perceptive administrations at least register them while the perceptive *and* proactive administrations lead such transformations. Very few economies of the world are blessed with these twin capabilities; most others need not despair, however. Not being in the forefront of revolutionary changes in the past does not mean that the country cannot be a leader in future, *provided that the nation has learnt from the past as to how to visualise and develop the future!*

India, despite its hoary history, had to take the bow of modern industrialisation only from the time of its independence in August 1947. Indian administration's cognitive skills, including those related to conceptualisation and analysis of industrial development, have started evolving in the 1950s and started laying the developmental pathways for industrial development from the 1960s. All through the period, there have been opportunities to witness and interpret as well as absorb and implement how other nations pursued their growth. India followed a mixed economy model and achieved mixed results until a crisis of immense proportions stared at the economy in the early 1990s. The period of liberalisation which commenced in 1992 was a period of enlightenment for economic and industrial planning. That said, it cannot be denied that some of the important foundations were laid prior to liberalisation while far more could have been done after liberalisation. Whether a nation merely views such transformational movements as products of time or makes such transformations happen proactively is a resultant of many factors. This chapter reviews five 'seed to tree' developments in India to examine if some lessons can be read out of them.

Fourth Industrial Revolution

Professor Klaus Schwab, Founder and the Executive Chairman of World Economic Forum explores in his book, *The Fourth Industrial Revolution* the technological changes that are occurring at an exponential pace and that could dramatically transform the way we live. He suggests breakthroughs in artificial intelligence, machine learning, quantum computing, 3D printing, nanotechnology, biotechnology, gene editing, mobile connectivity, wearables, Internet of Things, robotics, autonomous cars, renewable energy, materials sciences, space travel, and so on. He feels that there would be a confluence of physical, digital, and biological developments, with each development amplifying the others. He says that the World governments are yet to grasp the impact of the change in terms of the velocity of the change, the depth and breadth of the change, and the systems impact. He suggests that the transformation would connect billions more people digitally, increase organisational efficiencies, regenerate the natural environment, extend, and improve human ageing, and at least partially undo the damage of the past. He also is apprehensive that governments and organisations could fail to deploy and harness the benefits of new technologies appropriately, and could lead to new concerns of privacy, security and inequality, fragmenting and damaging the societies and nations further.

Engineering of the 1960s

For the global industrial economy, the 1960s represented the heydays of modernisation and expansion of traditional industries that represented the bulwark of a developed economy. A technologically resurgent Japan brought in new efficiencies to industries such as steel, automobiles, and capital goods, and laid the foundations of a globally networked production-consumption structure, which is based more on competitiveness than on national origin. For India, that period had coincided with the goal of self-reliance for some of the industries in the list such as steel, medium commercial vehicles and capital goods which became preferred choices, *albeit* with a heavy dependence on import of design and process technologies, equipment, and components from countries such as Russia, UK, and Germany. Unfortunately, the socialistic dogma of the Pandit Jawaharlal Nehru government served to shut out the development of other important growth engines such as automobiles and white goods.

The 1960s were notable for two concepts of indigenous development that new cities and economies could be built around new industries, and that more industries meant more economic power to States in India's federal development paradigm. Cities such as Bhilai, Rourkela, Bokaro, Jamshedpur, Dhanbad, and Durgapur stand testimony to the first concept. The now flourishing steel plants in far-flung Southern cities such as Visakhapatnam and Salem stand as living examples of the struggles by the States to get such steel plants. Youngsters were offered only three core engineering educational streams such as mechanical, electrical, and civil in the 1950s, keeping in view limited industrial perspectives. But that was also the time when in other developed countries of USA, Europe and Japan transistor radios and other electronics devices began to be manufactured in billions. Even as India built a solid traditional engineering infrastructure, the emerging electronics age got ignored by the country during the 1960s.

Electronics of the 1970s

The 1970s were verily the electronics age of computers, audio-video devices, home appliances and a host of electronics systems that provided better accuracy and repeatability to traditional capital goods. The 1970s also saw the emergence of software coding, from the punched card readers to machine languages to FORTRAN and such other languages for man-machine interface. The Indian ministers and bureaucrats probably knew that they were wrong in giving the global electronics revolution a miss in terms of indigenisation but did little to correct. When IIT Madras imported IBM 1401 mainframe computer in 1974 to support development of indigenous technologies, C Subramaniam, the learned Union Minister for Industrial Development remarked that imports of such sophisticated technologies was probably not the best way to develop the indigenous industry. In fact, the governments of that time allowed the free import of second hand or aged equipment to promote industrialisation (import of Innocenti scooter plant to set up Scooters India in Lucknow was one example!).

If China has, over the years, become the great manufacturing workshop of the world and the preferred manufacturing outsourcing destination, the seeds of that industrial 'Amazon' were sown in the late 1970s, when the concepts of market economy were first embraced in the late 1970s, and the foundations of mass consumer electronics industry began to be laid. While India started to introduce electronics and telecommunications as well as other diversified engineering courses, the country saw the flight of technical talent to USA and Europe which offered the new-age electro-mechanical and mechatronic industrial development. Continuing the inward looking traditional industrial policies, the socialistic ideologues, and governments of the 1970s began to add computers, consumer electronics and home appliances to the list of "luxury goods" that only automobiles and air conditioners represented till then! More than four decades later, even in 2013, the country was still not sure of being an electronics-driven industrial powerhouse like China has been from the 1980s.

Automobiles of the 1980s

Amidst the lag of India's industrial and economic competitiveness, something that was maverick happened in the 1980s – the establishment of Maruti Suzuki India Limited in 1981 by the Government of India in 50:50 joint venture partnership with Suzuki Motor Corporation of Japan! Maruti Suzuki verily ushered in an automobile revolution in India with an unprecedented influx of new passenger car models and micro-light commercial vehicles, mostly with Japanese technologies and their subsequent indigenisation. This has led to the progressive creation of four Detroit-like automobile hubs in India, one in the traditionally automobile oriented Chennai region, the second in the Northern Gurgaon region where Maruti Suzuki established itself, the third in the Western Pune region where Tata Motors and Bajaj Auto led the revolution, and now in the North-Western Sanand region, host to several firms well established in the other hubs. There were, of course, large two-wheeler and four-wheeler facilities in Jamshedpur, Nasik, Mumbai, Aurangabad, and certain other parts of the country.

The automobile industry of the 1980s played a major role in starting a new manufacturing revolution and a new automobile manufacturing clustering in India. With a production level of 25 million vehicles per year, India is one of the largest producers of automobiles in the world. In terms of two-wheelers, India is globally the largest with an output of 20 million vehicles. India is also the only large and structured player globally in the unique and ubiquitous three-wheeler segment with an output of 783,000 vehicles per annum. In cars (and utility vehicles) also, India is no longer a trailing country. From a meagre production of 30,000 till the late 1970s, India now clocks an output of 3.8 million! Commercial vehicles are also highly diversified and expanded with an annual output of 810,000. Performance on the export front has, however, been less than desirable. The only notable bright spot on the automotive export front has been the export of 2.3 million two-wheelers, constituting about 12 percent of the total two-wheeler output while all others have had insignificant (low single digit percentage) export levels.

Software of the 1990s

Even as automobiles began representing the new hardware of Indian industry from the 1980s, software emerged as the first driver of India's global competitiveness. The 1980s saw maturing of Tata Consultancy Services from punching to coding, and the founding of India's future software industry bellwether, Infosys. This phase represented the start of another type of migration of talent within India, from manufacturing to software! With the foundations laid in the 1980s, in the 1990s software came to be associated with a larger canvas of information technology (IT), emphatically transforming the way the world looked at India and software development. The sector also established that India's global delivery model could provide leadership not merely in terms of talent cost advantage but more in terms of seamless turnaround of systems development and transactions. IT has also laid the foundations of a new youthful middle-class society that began embracing consumer economy and driving products and services typical of such economy.

India's IT sector has been notable for a massive investment in in-house training and development, in terms of more up to date coding skills and multi-country linguistic and cultural approaches. The industry has perfected a model of twin recruitment and development engines driving scale and globalisation. After its global success, the IT industry has been trying to move up the value system by offering consultancy services and through vertical specialisations. These are, however, logical steps and do not constitute any strategic redefinition. A major failing of the Indian IT sector has been in terms of its disinclination towards strong inorganic growth and diffidence towards developing its own product platforms. It has taken a Vishal Sikka as the new CEO to try to add a strong product direction to Infosys over the last three years. Not many IT majors, however, seem inclined to commit resources for product investments. The future of the Indian IT industry is as strong as ever as a global IT service provider but probably below the potential in the current and emerging digital scenario.

Internet of the 2000s

The Internet has done wonders for globalisation and communication. The Internet of People connects people and organisations across the globe through a host of devices such as computers, tablets, and smart phones, through a telecommunications backbone. Many things that are done physically, from retailing to movie screening, began to be conducted by remote management through the Internet, in an increasing measure. After digital book publishing and reading, electronic commerce with fintech has become the new platform. This has resulted in a huge shift in how business is conducted in various fields, and the future potential. On an average, 11.82 lakh tickets were sold daily through IRCTC's Website and Mobile App during FY2022-23 which is still a fraction of 23 million passengers moving on any day over the Indian railway network. There could be an explosion of the Internet of People in India with better and universal broadband and Wi-Fi connectivity, lowering of tariffs for data transmission and availability of additional spectrum.

It is now getting evident that the next revolution on the Internet could be more profound. The Internet of Things could connect devices and environments in multiple ways, revolutionising how people live on a day-to-day basis. Healthcare, travel, home life, retailing are all set to become more real time and inclusive. RFIDs, sensors, scanners, software, analytics, processors, and telecommunications would determine if product and industrial structures would undergo a metamorphosis. Unfortunately, the greater the input of technological change the greater is also the level of waste. For example, as opposed to replacing normal electric bulbs or refrigerators after their useful life, technologically connected appliances may induce replacement every year as new technology arrives. The e-waste generated by smart phones and tablets is indicative of the waste that could occur across all product categories because of the device explosion pursuant to the Internet of Things.

Digital of the 2020s

The 2020s promise to take forward all the cumulative scientific and technological developments to a completely new level. Core scientific disciplines such as physics, chemistry, biology and mathematics, and core technological disciplines such as civil, mechanical, electrical, electronics, communication, and computers are getting merged as never before to create new disciplines of autonomy, clean energy, robotics, genetics, artificial intelligence, and the like. There are two aspects to the transformation of the 2020s – life and lifestyle. All the scientific and technological developments until recently focused only on lifestyle improvement through more products and services on one hand and higher resource generation and product consumption on the other. This overriding emphasis, driven by managerial approaches of hyper-competition, have pressured the planetary resources and the ecosystem almost near to a point of no return.

In this context, the digital technologies of 2020, which comprise physical, biological, and electronic integrated systems, are expected to usher in a change. Established and start-up companies are expected to find innovative solutions to do more with less. Controlling climate change and developing a circular economy are the two key tasks for the firms. However, this requires more enlightened managerial processes that balance corporate wealth maximisation with planetary health maximisation. This must also ensure that increased production and consumption benefit those at the bottom of the pyramid. Both these approaches call for new bodies of knowledge in science and technology, that are deployed by bold new and responsible methods of management. Figure 20.1 illustrates the impact of the Fourth Industrial Revolution.

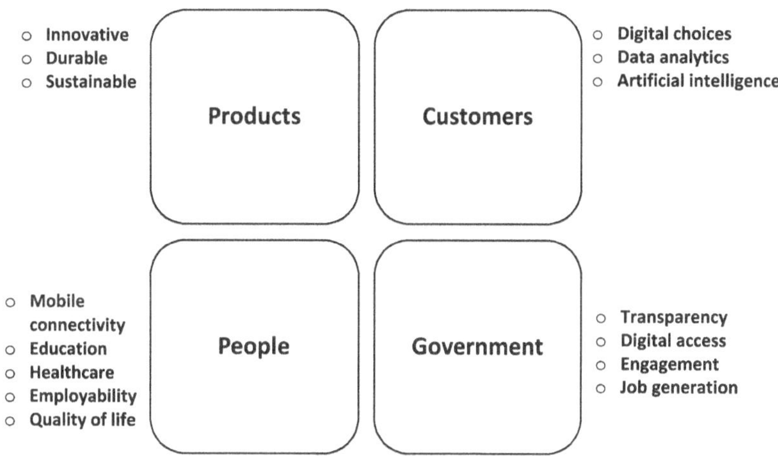

Figure 20.1: Impact of Fourth Industrial Revolution

Indigenous Seeds

The choice of just five sectors as above to describe India's industrial development of the last few decades is by no means comprehensive (for example, pharmaceuticals – a leading global industry of India – was not covered!) but is certainly illustrative. The seeds of India's industrial development have been from trees that have grown elsewhere. Even in respect of IT where India has become a global leader, not a single computer language or operating system has been developed in India (may have been developed elsewhere partially with Indian talent, however). The transhipped seeds, and in some cases the transplanted trees themselves, grew in the eager markets of India. Over the last several decades, there have been gallant efforts to indigenise design and manufacture; yet even the new NDA government's current manufacturing paradigm of 'Make in India' seems to require overseas seeds. The experience suggests that financial investments, technologies, equipment, and components come in bundles each with a cycle of cautious investment, domestic consumption, limited exports, and capital repatriation with a time span in mind. Every time industrial renewal is desired, the cycle of imported seeds *et al* repeats itself.

With the Modi government firmly committed to a policy of India's economic growth equating with India's self-respect, a different seeding programme for industrial and economic growth is required. India now has the option of staging the next manufacturing revolution following the previous model or improving upon it to make it a self-perpetuating cycle of indigenous development. For this to happen, a new genre of seeds is required. The past industrial revolutions were hamstrung by limited scientific and technological educational streams which came into existence only after the development of physical industrial infrastructure. This has resulted in talent bottlenecks and skill gaps.

A bolder India must create educational disciplines far in advance of the sighting of new industrial infrastructure. If necessary, to cut the developmental times short, the vast Indian diaspora which is enthralled by the prospect of a New India must be encouraged to come on two-to-three-year sabbatical to seed their talents in Indian industry, research laboratories, and educational institutions. More importantly, 'Make in India' paradigm must be supplemented by 'Research in India', and 'Design in India' paradigms. And, as the costly lesson of missing the electronics revolution shows, no sunrise sector should be ignored by India in this phase.

India and Industrial Revolutions

Despite being a pioneer in science, technology, and medicine in the early centuries (more than 20 discoveries from number systems to surgical procedures and from Ayurveda to astrology), India has been a mere follower in the first three industrial revolutions. The First Industrial Revolution commenced in 1784 with main characteristics/products of steam, water, and mechanical production equipment. In 1870, the Second Industrial Revolution started with electricity and division of labour and mass production. The Third Industrial Revolution commenced in 1969 with electronics, information technology and automated production. As contrasted with the first three industrial revolutions which had a time span of around 100 years in each case between them, the Fourth Industrial Revolution took less than fifty years to emerge with a unique fusion of cyber, physical, and biological systems. This is a unique opportunity to move from being a mere follower to an innovator and a differentiator in some of the drivers of the Fourth Industrial Revolution. Opportunities abound in robotics, artificial intelligence, machine learning, deep learning, augmented reality, virtual reality, blockchains, autonomous driving, space travel, immune-therapy and engineered biology, to quote a few. Figure 20.2 summarises the industrial revolutions.

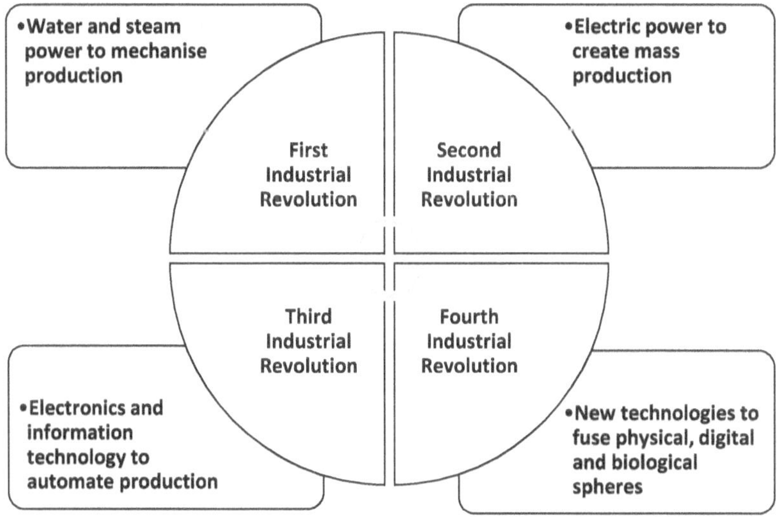

Figure 20.2: Summary of the Industrial Revolutions

Chapter 21

Beyond Microeconomics and Macroeconomics

The Need for Indian Social Economics

Economics is a fascinating social science that has accompanied the industrial revolutions. The first formal organisation of economic thought, *albeit* in a political setting, is attributed to Adam Smith (1776) for his book "An Enquiry into the Nature and Causes of the Wealth of Nations". Alfred Marshall's textbook "Principles of Economics" (1890) laid the foundation to the microeconomic branch of economics. The adverse economics of the Great Depression of the 1930s spurred the development of macroeconomic thought. John Maynard Keynes' book "The General Theory of Employment, Interest and Money" published in 1936 provided new perspectives of macroeconomic thought. Over the years, almost every aspect of human endeavour got its own economics perspectives, from industrial economics to welfare economics, for example. Microeconomics and macroeconomics, however, continue to be the more dominant streams of economics to date.

Microeconomics deals with the economic behaviour of individual markets, firms, entities, and individuals, focusing on matters such as, but not limited to, production, cost, scale and efficiency; supply, demand and equilibrium; scarcities, surpluses and elasticity of demand and supply, costs and prices, and theories of firm and industrial organisation. Macroeconomics deals with the issues of economy from the top, focusing on matters such as national income and output;

jobs and unemployment; price inflation and deflation; savings, investment, and consumption. Flow of money and business cycles as well as economic growth, international trade and international finance are some of the other considerations. It studies the impact of monetary policy and fiscal policy. Monetary policy is implemented by the central banks to control the liquidity in the economic system to ensure economic stability. Fiscal policy relates to the use by the governments of revenues and expenditures, along with savings and taxes to influence economic growth. More importantly, climate policies impact social economics and behaviours.

Climate Change and Social Economics

Much of socio-economic thought and action focuses on economics that directly influences the lives of poor, be it in terms of job creation, subsidies, or loans. An important school of thought that has emerged is that industrial and economic actions impact environment adversely, leading to climate changes that hit vulnerable sections of the population hard. A United Nations Report, *The World Economic and Social Survey 2016: Climate Change Resilience – an Opportunity for Reducing Inequalities* suggested that transformative governmental policies could do a lot to address the inequalities through climate actions. According to the Report, billions of people are affected by weather-related disasters which are caused by environmental degradation. The economic cost is estimated at 5 percent of GDP. It speaks of a vicious cycle whereby population groups affected by structural inequalities live in the least desirable land prone to the ravages of the nature thus suffering the maximum damage and requiring additional economic costs to redress the suffering. The suggested action, requiring billions of dollars in focused investments, is two-fold: resilience to climate change through better predictive and corrective technologies, and transformative policies to root out established structural inequalities.

Indian Scenario

India, ever since its independence in 1947, has been following established economic theories to drive economic growth. The socialistic pattern of development curtailed free market economics until 1991 but the macroeconomic liberalisation thereafter gave a new upward drift to the Indian economy. Regardless of the economic system, monetary policy followed by the Reserve Bank of India and announced in its periodic policy reviews, and the fiscal policy followed by the Central government and effected through the annual union budgets influenced the investment and consumption patterns of the society. The sensitivity of the markets to banking liquidity and interest rates and to tax and allocation policies has been only increasing with years. In addition, annual budget-related and periodic context-based economic reforms, and policy stimulation measures, including export-import policies, industrial development policies, and poverty alleviation programmes exert significant socio-economic impact.

India has been home to some of the sharpest economic brains. Amartya Sen, Amit Mitra, Arvind Panagariya, Ashok Desai, Bibek Debroy, Bimal Jalan, C Rangarajan, D R Gadgil, D Subbarao, I G Patel, J C Kumarappa, Jagdish Bhagwati, Jairam Ramesh, Kaushik Basu, Manmohan Singh, Montek Singh Ahluwalia, Nanabhoy Palkhiwala, Omkar Goswami, P C Mahalanobis, Raghuram Rajan, Subramanian Swamy, V K R V Rao, Y K Alagh, and Y V Reddy are some of the well-known names. Several political leaders including Jawaharlal Nehru, the first Prime Minister of independent India, and several finance ministers from C D Deshmukh and T T Krishnamachari of the yesteryears to Arun Jaitley and Nirmala Sitharaman of current years have been economically savvy leaders. Narendra Modi, Prime Minister has fine economic awareness and perspicacity which is reflected not only in his many passionate speeches but also in several innovative programmes of the Government. Mahatma Gandhi, the father of the nation, had articulated his unique brand of

Gandhian economics targeted at economic self-sufficiency and growth of cottage and small industries which is relevant even today. Figure 21.1 illustrates the Indian scenario since 1947.

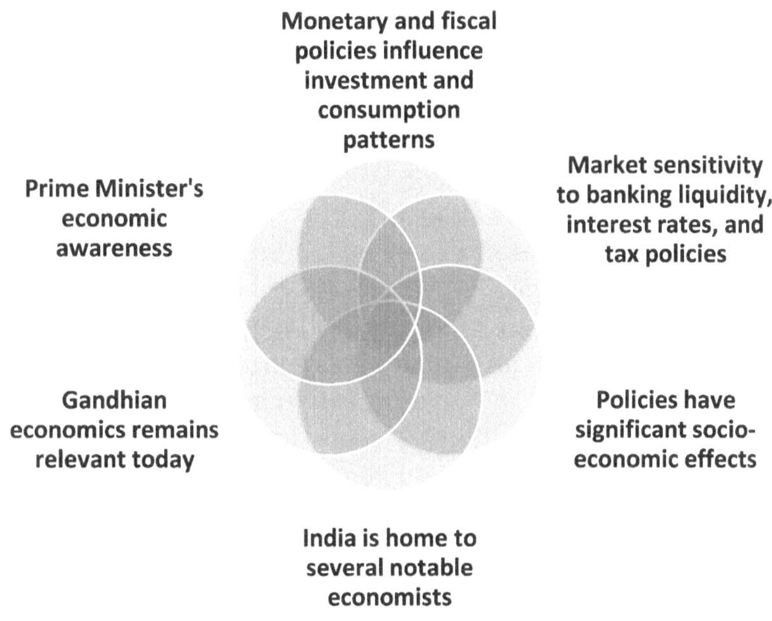

Figure 21.1: Indian Scenario since 1947

Intriguing India

Although the phrase "Incredible India" has been coined only a few years ago, India had always been incredible. The scientific and technical thought that went into the centuries' old Indian heritage of Ayurveda, Yoga, Astronomy, and Architecture (especially temple and palace architecture) was indeed phenomenal. Post-independence too, India demonstrated rare pluck to construct its own massive dams, build its own heavy industry, establish its own banks and financial institutions, develop its own educational infrastructure, and create its own aerospace infrastructure. India may not have gained global competitiveness, but the country certainly acquired the capability for self-reliance and self-sufficiency across a range of basic and heavy industries that is rare amongst the emerging markets. In all this, adoption of micro and macroeconomics to an Indian context, in a somewhat serendipitous manner, played a role. India's development may have lagged its true potential, but a base has certainly been laid for more accelerated development if right constructs are developed and relied upon.

At the same time, India has indeed been an intriguingly bipolar country characterised, for example, by paradoxes such as massive educational level but meagre skill level, strong penchant for growth but constraints all the way, vibrant democratic culture but strong vestiges of feudalism, and phenomenal wealth generation in pockets but continued prevalence of poverty in broad swathes. Economic growth with social equity has been the avowed objective of parties and governments alike but togetherness in fulfilling the 'growth with equity' objective has been missing. The paradox of incredible growth potential constrained by intriguing plurality of thought makes one wonder if India can benefit to the requisite degree only by Western economic thought or would require a distinctly Indian economic construct that is tailor-made to solve indigenous socio-economic problems but without losing the global context. Even issues like quantitative stimulus or directed subsidies are not discussed and framed with objective economic thought that addresses India's issues in a customised manner.

Success Factors

As discussed in the several chapters of this book, India's success would lie in enhancing the knowledge base to power multiple growth drivers. These include enhancing agricultural productivity with sustainable crop economics, improving technological innovation with rapid commercialisation, developing infrastructural sinews with meaningful capital productivity, expanding manufacturing capacities with global competitiveness, rural and urban renewal with protection of ownership interests, creation of jobs with minimal migration pains, ensuring universal housing, sanitation, education, and healthcare to all, just to state a few. Economic policies and administrative actions of the successive governments have tried to provide policies and budgets with incentives and subsidies to tackle some of the above needs individually, depending on the political perspectives. Most of these have been based on established macroeconomic and microeconomic approaches which are buffered by Indian socio-economic and cultural compulsions. Given that all these cumulatively have not helped India reach its full potential, it is time that economic models that specifically address India's development concerns are created.

India's socio-economic needs would require an Indian social economics theory (and practice) that addresses the typically Indian issues of (i) agrarian economics, (ii) infrastructure economics, (iii) Make in India economics, (iv) Research in India economics, (v) renewal economics, (vi) employment economics, (vii) migration economics, and (viii) behavioural economics. As illustrated in Figure 21.2, these are critical levers that define India's social economics.

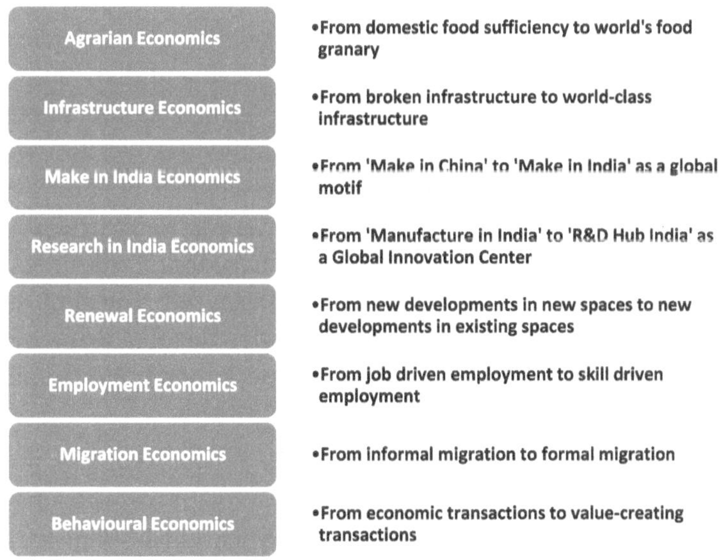

Figure 21.2: Key Levers in India's Social Economics

The reason for focussing on the first seven aspects is obvious; if well-researched and well-modelled economic theory is developed on these aspects, not only better economic policies that stimulate gross domestic product and higher per capita income can be developed but also, they can be better implemented with widespread support. These aspects which are independent as well as integrated can together provide better socio-economic development in the country. All of these will, however, need to be supported by a solid understanding of Indian behavioural economics with perspectives that are regional as well as national. The eight branches of Indian social economics are discussed below.

(i) Agrarian Economics

India, despite decades of industrial development and the recent burgeoning of service economy, is still an agrarian economy. The potential for capacity expansion and productivity in agricultural production and distribution is impacted by crop economics on one hand and irrigation economics on the other. Economic models which assess the impact of crop mix on food grain and commodity self-sufficiency and the impact of dams on year-round crop patterns are required. The microeconomics of India's debt-ridden small farmer is affected by spot prices and distribution margins. While farm subsidies mitigate the burden to some extent, an in-depth study of crop economics for individual and national sustainability is required. Similarly, the economics of dams and reservoirs are also poorly understood. There is no reason why major irrigation projects like Polavaram (in Andhra Pradesh) had to hang fire for decades. There is also no reason why interlinking of at least a few rivers should not be initiated nationally. Economic modelling of irrigation projects could stimulate better allocations or encourage setting up of special purpose vehicles.

(ii) Infrastructure Economics

That India has lagged all the developed nations and key emerging economies in infrastructure development is well known. The NDA government has admitted that the public-private collaboration model has not had much impact and needs redefinition. Most private sector infrastructure firms carry huge levels of debt from public sector banks. The economics of infrastructure development in the Indian context are unique with long lead times and slow returns even after project completion. From the project conceptualisation stage through the project appraisal stage, the economics of each infrastructure project need to be understood not merely in terms of the internal rate of return for the project but the overall economic uplift because of the multiplier effects of infrastructure projects. The NDA government has tried to break this jinx through ambitious roadbuilding and waterway development projects (Bharatmala and Sagarmala, respectively), as also futuristics logistics project (Gati Shakti), The study of infrastructure engineering and management should be a special branch of microeconomics while budgeting of such projects should be a special branch of macroeconomics with appropriate monitory and fiscal policies to support.

(iii) *Make in India Economics*

With India's low wage costs, large talent pool, frugal engineering, and mass mobilisation capabilities, the world should embrace Prime Minister Narendra Modi's Make in India mantra enthusiastically. Narendra Modi Government wants India to move into the manufacture of the latest generation products such as electric vehicles, electric batteries, solar modules, green hydrogen, semiconductors, drones, telecom gear, and so on, with Aatmanirbharata as the theme. India should propose objectively to the investors the sources of economic advantage of Make in India strategy in respect of each industrial activity. India should also propose for itself the role of India's large domestic market in leading to globally competitive production. Typical economic thought teaches us that high-end niche products subsidise low-end mass products. In the Indian economic milieu, it could be the other way around; India's bottom of the pyramid can provide huge scale economics which can be leveraged for global products. Tata

Motors' success with JLR is a corporate level economic behaviour of this theorem of domestic strength supporting an overseas turnaround. There is a need for a more rigorous understanding and agile execution of the Make in India economics for a greater success of the initiative.

(iv) Research in India Economics

It is less recognised globally, and even in India, that India can provide greater advantages through Research in India projects. Globally competitive Research and Development (R&D) is time- and cost- intensive. Fundamental discoveries and inventions are, in addition, uncertain. The effort and resource to outcome and commercialization ratios are very high. In the pharmaceutical industry, for example, hundreds and thousands of experimentations are required for arriving at a candidate molecule, component, or product. India with its vast pool of talented scientists and engineers can make a difference to the global R&D of Indian and transnational firms. India needs to develop state-of-the-art research parks that can employ researchers in millions and deploy resources in billions of dollars. Each such park must have its IPR and patenting office. Such an infrastructure will certainly give a fillip to Indian enterprise to set up organic and contract research organisations in a big way. Such a research ecosystem will also attract transnational firms to set up their bases in India.

(v) Renewal Economics

India has an enormous need, and hence offers immense potential, for rural and urban renewal. There is no habitat that can be excluded from the renewal paradigm. Yet, renewal is not easy in India. The way the previous government of Andhra Pradesh failed to build a new capital on a zero base as a multibillion-dollar venture at Amaravathi and how the subsequent government failed to develop Visakhapatnam as a capital-qualifying region is proof of the developmental needs that are not being met by the current approaches. However, as illustrated by the same examples, any distributed renewal or new development – urban or rural – has several implications for overrunning current land use and community avocation practices, despite such renewal being essential. On the face of it, continuous renewal offers the most economical way of developing habitats in a distributed manner relative to big bang new constructions. Only when the economics of renewal are understood can the overall spatial planning in India, including development of smart cities and smart villages, be brought to global standards, consistent with the Indian socio-economic imperatives.

(vi) *Employment Economics*

For India's democracy to function effectively, it must address the pressing issue of unemployment. Historically, India has experienced fluctuating unemployment rates, typically ranging between 5 percent and 10 percent. As of December 2023, India's unemployment rate stood at 8.7 percent, which is higher than the Euro region's rate of 6.4 percent. Additionally, India's unemployment rate surpasses that of Western developed countries such as the United States and the United Kingdom, where unemployment rates are 3.5 percent and 4.2 percent, respectively. When compared to Asian developed nations like China and South Korea, with rates of 5.2 percent and 2.8 percent, respectively, India faces a higher unemployment challenge.

More than gross employment, underemployment, and over-employment as well as skill-need gaps are causes for concern. Underemployment is characterised by people performing jobs of lower level than they are capable of (for example, just digging trenches rather than building reservoirs). Overemployment is characterised by more people than required performing the same job (for example, three or more people manning a toll plaza post). Skill gap is characterised by an individual failing to work to a national or international standard (for example, a painter failing to prepare a surface prior to painting or a carpenter failing to provide smooth edges and finishes). The elimination of underemployment and overemployment and investment for skill development have economic implications that need a uniquely Indian thought. Several of the domain-economics initiatives discussed earlier would boost employment in India. Educational institutions must play their part by driving up employability.

(vii) *Migration Economics*

Urbanisation is a concomitant of economic development, universally. Migration of people from rural areas to urban areas is also a natural accompanying phenomenon. However, unplanned, and under-resourced migration causes urban squalor and triggers urban unrest. India has two additional dimensions - of people migrating from States of lower per capita income or lower economic activity to other States perceived to be better, and people leaving distressed farm jobs in search of perceived urban opportunities. The economics of migration tend to be mirages when people chase minimal employment with marginal wages far away from their homes. Arbitrage migration could pose great risks when emergencies strike; for example, Covid-19 related lockdowns caused massive reverse migration, and it took months to recover for industrial and business undertakings, even after Covid ebbed. Real economics would occur when economic activity moves into regions where people reside and touch their lives directly. Large scale industrialisation or large-scale mining of natural resources with necessary caveats is one solution. More importantly, such underdeveloped regions should be stimulated with a small and micro enterprise start-up culture that brings soft economic touch to indigenous evolution and promotes self-sustainability. It must be a form of Gandhian Economics whereby the well-to-do regions/entities (downtown metros, factories, businesses, and offices), and people (industrialists and businessmen) act as trustees for the underdeveloped regions (be it, Bastar forests, Idukki riverbed or Manyam agencies). Migration economics needs to be a uniquely Indian requirement.

(viii) Behavioural Economics

Behavioural economics is the study of the impact of psychological, social, emotional, and cultural factors on economic decisions made by individuals and institutions, and the consequences for microeconomic and macroeconomic factors like costs, prices, savings, and investments. Standard economic theory suggests that if individuals understand the economic consequences of their decisions, they take decisions that are in their best self-interests. The reality is that individuals (and even institutions) suffer from biases and transient perceptions, and do not necessarily have self-awareness, self-control, and objectivity. Given the plurality of the Indian society and the lack of insightful literacy for vast sections of population (at all levels of the population pyramid) and the divisive nature of political discourse, economic decisions tend to be inappropriately made or even appropriate decisions tend to get stalled. We have seen earlier that there is a paucity of economic theories that are tuned to India's indigenous problems. This inadequacy coupled with the vast mosaic of Indian behaviours makes it mandatory that an Indian version of behavioural economics is urgently developed.

Indian Social Economics

The country needs an integrated Indian social economics thought which applies all the established disciplines of economics including, in the main, micro and macroeconomics, and develops economic principles and theories that are uniquely relevant to India. Such indigenous thought would enhance capacities, capabilities, and effectiveness in the areas of agriculture, infrastructure, manufacturing, renewal, employment, migration, and behaviours. These are typically Indian issues on which everyone is agreed in terms of the overarching goal of economic growth with social equity. However, lack of directed and issue-specific economic thought has prevented due progress and fulfilment of potential. India does have its general and applied schools of economics. Every premier college or institution has a department of economics. There are also specialised institutions like Madras School of Economics, National Council for Applied Economic Research (NCAER), Institute for Social and Economic Change and so on.

The established schools and centres, however, have not been focussed on analysing economic issues that need to be specifically addressed in India. Nor has there been an effort to develop economic principles that guide public policy and governance at central and state levels. While several case studies have been brought out, there has been no specific vision to develop an India-specific economic theory. Intellectuals and administrators are more focused on variations in known policy measures and instruments rather than on developing India-specific prescriptions. Now that the NDA government is keen to establish new centres of higher education and research, and the States are also keen to participate in such higher educational initiatives, it would be appropriate to establish Indian Institutes of Social Economics and Research in the principal geographical regions of the country to develop India-specific economic thought and practice with a board of economists who have passion and commitment for all things that are Indian and indigenous. Such institutions must be multi-disciplinary with experts outside of economics as well to address the needs of the eight categories of economics discussed herein. Economic Survey 2017-18 has drawn attention to the behavioural preference of the Indian society to sons, and the need to correct that.

Meta Behavioural Bias

India needs social transformation on several dimensions but getting rid of the deeply ingrained bias against the girl child and women is one of the most needed behavioural correctives. Laying a special emphasis on gender and son meta-preference, the Economic Survey 2017-18 suggests that the country should commit itself to gender equality and empowerment of women. Pointing out that participation of women in the country's workforce has declined from 36 percent in 2005-06 to 24 percent in 2015-16, the Survey advocates the importance of increasing opportunities for women in education and employment. Traditionally, women have a role in agricultural work but without any entitlements. Recent NDA Government's flagship schemes like "Beti Bachao Beti Padhao" and "Sukanya Samridhi Yojana" focus on formal sectors. It is important that there should be programmes that integrate, reward, and incentivise women as part of agricultural economy too. Though the Government has earmarked 30 percent of the budget allocation for women beneficiaries in all ongoing schemes, programmes and development activities, there needs to be a more potent driver of women participation. India's social transformation would rest verily on women equality, at all stages. Similarly, major efforts are required to ensure that girls are brought into and retained in the schooling system by ensuring access, safety, comfort, and convenience for the school children. By maximising the enrolment rate and minimising the dropout rate for girl children, gender equality can be ensured.

Chapter 22

Creating India's Own Space

The Amazing Upward Journey of Indian Space Research Organisation (ISRO)

If one futuristic indigenous endeavour of India has been taken note of by the entire world, it is India's space endeavour. From 1969, India's Indian Space Research Organisation has been conducting space missions. However, India's Chandrayaan-3 which landed our own Vikram Lander and Pragyan Rover on the South Pole of the Moon on August 23, 2023, got India global admiration. In fact, India is the first and only nation that soft-landed a vehicle on the South Pole of the Moon. This has been quickly followed up with Aditya L1 mission, India's first space-based mission to study the Sun. The spacecraft was planned to be placed in a halo orbit around the Lagrange Point 1 (L1) of the Sun-Earth system, which is about 1.5 million km from the Earth, which has been achieved. A satellite placed in the halo orbit around the L1 point has the major advantage of continuously viewing the Sun without any occultation/eclipses.

On October 21, 2023 the Gaganyaan mission achieved a successful rocket launch from Sriharikota by ISRO scientists. The mission, crucial for crew safety, attained precise results, including the successful separation of the Crew Module and Crew Escape components. A few other launches, including an ambitious project for study of Venus are also planned. These missions point to India's ingenuity and innovation, from concept to execution. These missions also underline the enterprising nature of India's space organisation, ISRO, and the Government of India. In consonance with the objective of this book in terms of understanding the performance and potential of India as a Knowledge Society, ISRO is an amazing case study. While there are many other organisations in India's public and private sectors that have developed and demonstrated globally competitive technologies (for example, Bhabha Atomic Research Centre, Hindustan Aeronautics, Bharat Electronics, Cochin Shipyard, Larsen & Toubro, Tata Steel, Tata Motors, and Ashok Leyland), ISRO is certainly the top jewel in India's crown of indigenous technologies.

ISRO

The Indian Space Research Organisation (ISRO), a wholly owned entity of the Government of India came into being in 1969, taking over the space programme of Indian National Committee for Space Research (INCOSPAR) that was established in 1962. Dr Vikram Sarabhai, the eminent space scientist, was the driving force behind both INCOSPAR and ISRO. Over the decades, ISRO has established that Indian organisations can excel in scientific and technological accomplishments of the highest order. It dispels the myth that high talent gravitates towards only high salaries offered by the private sector. It also dispels the myth that cutting edge science and technology cannot be developed indigenously by India. It also establishes that India has broad-based scientific technological leadership that can lead the complex space missions; from Vikram Sarabhai of the 1960s to K Sivan of 2018, several scientific and technological leaders helmed the great institution to consistently higher glories. ISRO's achievements are not infrequent; in fact, from the date of establishment in 1969, ISRO has been clocking a string of achievements. If at all, the pace and scope of ISRO achievements only accelerated in the 2000s.

As of March 2023, ISRO has fulfilled 125 spacecraft missions, 92 launch missions, 13 student satellites, 2 re-entry missions, 431 foreign satellites of 34 countries. Its spacecraft range covers a wide range of communication satellites, earth observation satellites, scientific spacecraft, navigation satellites, experimental satellites, small satellites, and student satellites.

Starting with SLV and ASLV launchers, ISRO developed a wide range of launchers called PSLV, GSLV and sounding rockets. The futuristic range of launchers includes HRLV, SSLV, RLV-TD, Scramjet Engine - TD. The applications include earth observation, satellite communications, disaster management, satellite navigation, and climate and environment. It has 19 laboratories, including Vikram Sarabhai Space Centre and Satish Dhawan Space Centre. ISRO has more than 20,000 employees, of which the Scientific & technical manpower is about 75 percent of the total manpower. Figure 22.1 illustrates ISRO's key achievements and operations.

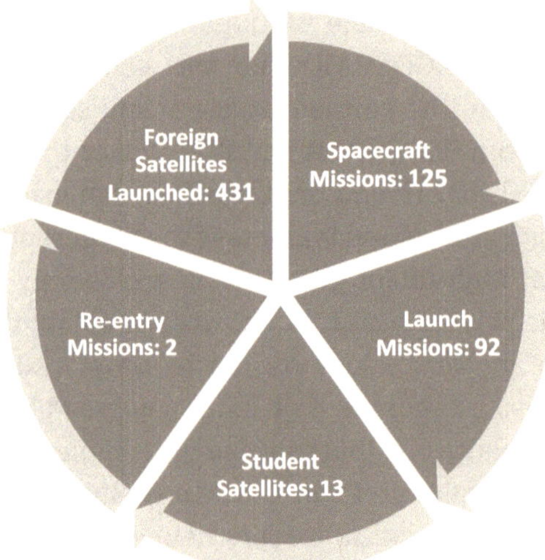

Figure 22.1: ISRO: Key Achievements and Operations

Competency and Cost

ISRO's competence has been established by its ability to send missions to Moon and Mars, and the plans to send missions to Jupiter and Venus. It has established a world record in February 2017 by launching 104 satellites of different countries through its PSLV. More recently, it has successfully tested the GSLV rocket, GSAT-11, capable of handling higher tonnage satellite payloads (4T). India's heaviest communication satellite was launched in December 2018. Many PSLV and GSLV launches were made between 2019 and 2022. In the first eight months of 2023, ISRO clocked one launch per month. With such accomplishments, and plans to master heavy payload launch technology, ISRO has rolled out a pathway for commercial space business. It has also achieved success in developing reusable launch vehicles and space shuttles which are essential for commercial space travel as attempted by private space organisations in US like Amazon and Virgin.

Global Space Agencies

India is among the Top 5 space agencies of the World, the other four being NASA of USA, CNSA of China, ESA of European inter-governmental cooperation, and RosCosmos of Russia. ISRO has an annual budget of USD 1.93 billion dollars, compared to USD 7.54 billion of ESA, USD 3.8 billion of RosCosmos and USD 25.4 billion of NASA. Yet, in terms of accomplishments, ISRO is well positioned to cater to global space business. Global space economy was at USD 464 billion in 2022, according to *The Space Report 2022*, published by Space Foundation. The four areas of business potential for ISRO seem to be in global demand for space data and applications, physical space products and launch services, and US and non-US governmental budgets. Training and reskilling of workforce could be another opportunity. The global space industry may reach an inflection point if point-to-point reusable space shuttles become commercially feasible.

India's space programmes are characterised by extremely low costs, compared to global norms. A PSLV programme of ISRO is accomplished at USD 15 million compared to USD 100 million that an Atlas launch programme requires. ISRO's Mangalyan Mars mission cost USD 73 million, far less than USD 671 million spent by US NASA on a similar mission. (The Hollywood movie 'Gravity' cost USD 100 million to make, as a comparison!). Chandrayaan-3 mission cost ISRO USD 74 million (Rs 615 crore) while the US NASA is expected to spend as much as USD 93 billion for its moon exploration programme Artemis by 2025.

Lower costs of indigenous hardware, research and people do contribute to the lower costs of the programme, but there is a unique Indian way of managing the space programmes that leads to the lower costs. Frugality, of course, should never be at the cost of safety, and ISRO has put in place systems to ensure that ISRO excels in not only launch competence but also safety and compliance.

Leadership Lessons

ISRO offers several lessons on achieving entity leadership in a technologically complex domain, and the role of human leadership in supporting such entity leadership. ISRO had, from the early inception, worked on an unflinching vision to harness space technology for national development, while pursuing space science research and planetary exploration. The vision was sought to be accomplished through several missions, each of which continued to evolve contemporaneously. It put in place robust systems for recruiting and developing scientists and engineers who share the mission and passion for space technology. The political and governmental apparatus insulated the organisation from the usual polemical and bureaucratic dynamics. The Space Commission fulfilled a purpose of harmony and synergy in this aspect.

The superlative aspect of ISRO relates to the scientific and technological leadership it has had from the inception. The current chairman, S. Somnath, under whose leadership ISRO has been having certain stellar space launches, has an illustrious set of predecessor leaders: Dr K. Sivan (2018-2022), A S Kiran Kumar (2015-2018), Dr K Radhakrishnan (2009-2014), Shri G Madhavan Nair (2003-2009), Dr K Kasturirangan (1994-2003), Prof U Ramachandra Rao (1984-1994), Prof Satish Dhawan (1972-1984), Prof M G K Menon (Jan-Sept 1972), and Dr Vikram Sarabhai (1963-1971). The seamless consistency and continuity in mission fulfilments and launches across the generations of brilliant leaders is instructive; it points to the fact that ISRO has been able to develop a committed and competent talent pool that can deliver. In fact, the current chairman S Somanath, and his predecessors K Sivan and Kiran Kumar have been homegrown ISRO veterans for decades.

ISRO also has been a clear leader in multiple technologies and in networking multiple locations. It has been a classic case of a national ambition becoming an economic force, years and decades later. The space research programmes were initiated by Dr Vikram Sarabhai in the early 1960s when applications using satellites were getting developed, and the space technology was the exclusive preserve of developed nations of the USA and USSR. From selective collaborations, ISRO soon became a developer of indigenous technology. ISRO is a prime example of vision-strategy-execution trilogy being the principal platform of growth in industry, infrastructure, and economy. Figure 22.2 summarises the leadership lessons from ISRO's success.

Figure 22.2: Leadership Lessons from ISRO's Success

Space Economics

ISRO runs on an annual budget (2023) of Rs 1.93 billion (USD 1.4 billion) which is humble relative to USD 25.4 billion allocated to US NASA. Yet, ISRO has been able to conduct multiple missions, quantitatively more than NASA! The World has started taking note of India's technologically advanced and cost-competitive space programme. While satellite launches and other space services for other countries could recover around half of the government's investments on ISRO, the economic benefits of ISRO's space leadership are far greater. They extend from the cost economics of self-reliance in a number of satellite-based services, and the spin-off benefits to other sectors of the Indian economy. For example, the battery technology (and the batteries) developed by ISRO that has powered US Mars mission can now power the ambitious goal of the Government of India to have an all-electric vehicle automobile industry by 2030.

It is important that the various sectors, industries, and enterprises that operate in, and contribute to, the Indian economy follow and excel in the model of growth pioneered by ISRO. The scientific, technological, operational, and leadership models of ISRO need to be researched further and developed as role models for other sectors. The governments also should appreciate how vision, missions as well as enterprise empowerment with due oversight (example, the Space commission) could energise enterprises. Leaders also should appreciate the importance of vision-strategy-execution trilogy, and the essentiality of institutionalising talent. The economy will be only as strong as its constituent sectors. ISRO illustrates how India can create its own unique space in the competitive global canvas.

ISRO: Service Provider or Industry?

Even robust research and data-based endeavour such as Economic Survey has probably failed to present and analyse the great achievements of ISRO in proper perspective. ISRO operations involve huge research and manufacturing activity on mega-industrial scale. ISRO contributes to national development through the application of space technology, comprising communication, navigation, and earth observation. ISRO operations help all sectors of the economy, from social development to strategic marksmanship. ISRO is a shining beacon for R&D innovation and self-reliance for India.

Bibliography

Brandenburger, Adam, and Barry Nalebuff. "Co-opetition: A Revolution Mindset That Combines Competition and Cooperation," 1996.

C. B. Rao. "Competitive Strategy: A Contemporary Retake," Notion Press, 2016.

C. B. Rao. "Leadership for India Inc.: An Experiential Treatise", Notion Press, 2017.

C. B. Rao. "Product Strategy and Corporate Success: Concepts and Cases from the Indian Automobile Industry," Notion Press, 2019

Economic Survey 2017-18. Ministry of Finance, New Delhi, 2018

Economic Survey 2022-23. Ministry of Finance, New Delhi, 2023.

Global Innovation Index, WIPO, 2023

Global Communication Platform. "Taiwan's Two Trillion, Twin Star (T3S) Plan," https://glocom.org./tech_reviews/geti/20020906_geti_s22/index.html

International patent applications defy 2022 challenges, continue upward trend, WIPO: https://www.wipo.int/pressroom/en/articles/2023/article_0002.html

Marshall, Alfred. "Principles of Economics," 1890.

Ministry of Education. National Education Policy 2020. https://www.education.gov.in

Ministry of Education releases All India Survey on Higher Education (AISHE): https://pib.gov.in

Mukherjee, Mita, "IIT course flexibility - Freedom to pursue another subject for up to 4 years." Telegraph India, 2014, https://www.telegraphindia.com/west-bengal/iit-course-flexibility-freedom-to-pursue-another-subject-for-up-to-4-years/cid/169160.

OECD, *Local Economic Leadership,* 2015.

Porter, Michael E. "Competitive Strategy: Techniques for Analyzing Industries and Competitors." Free Press, 1980.

Rao, Kembai Srinivasa. "Twin Balance Sheet Problem to Twin Balance Sheet Advantage." *Kembai Speaks, The Times of India*, 29 June 2023.

Reddy, Y. V. *K L N Prasad Memorial Lecture*, 2018.

Reserve Bank of India. "Financial Stability Report," June 2023

Schwab, Klaus. "The Fourth Industrial Revolution," 22 February 2017.

Smith, Adam. "An Enquiry into the Nature and Causes of the Wealth of Nations," 1776.

United Nations. "The World Economic and Social Survey 2016: Climate Change Resilience – an Opportunity for Reducing Inequalities." 2016.

US companies drive 2023 drug launches positioned for blockbuster success by 2028. *Pharmaceutical Technology*, May 30, 2023.

Vanderbilt University. *Dialogues Clinical Neurosciences*, vol. 8, no. 3, 2006, pp. 335-44.

World Intellectual Property Organization. "Technology Transfer, Intellectual Property and Effective University-Industry Partnerships: The Experience of China, India, Japan, Philippines, The Republic of Korea, Singapore and Thailand," 2007.

About the Author

Dr. C. Bhaktavatsala Rao received his Ph.D. Degree in Industrial Management and M. Tech. Degree in Industrial Engineering from the Indian Institute of Technology Madras, Chennai. He received his B.E. Degree in Mechanical Engineering from Sri Venkateswara University, Tirupati.

Dr. C. B. Rao has over forty-nine years of diversified experience in strategic and operational leadership of large, reputed companies, including global multinational corporations, in India. Dr. C. B. Rao's last formal assignment was as Managing Director/Executive Chairman of Hospira Healthcare India Pvt Limited, a Pfizer Company. Dr. Rao is a prolific writer with several publications in economic and business dailies and refereed journals. Dr Rao is the founder of LeaderCrest Academy. This book is the sixteenth in the series of books authored and published by Dr. Rao under his LeaderCrest Banner over the last seven years.

Dr C. B. Rao serves as Ajit Singhvi Chair Professor in the Department of Management Studies, Indian Institute of Technology Madras, Chennai. He is non-executive director on the boards of select companies. He also serves as adviser to global corporations.

www.ingramcontent.com/pod-product-compliance
Lightning Source LLC
Chambersburg PA
CBHW060534160726
47991CB00001B/312